BASEBALL
ACCESS®

Richard Saul Wurman

ACCESSPRESS Ltd.

What smartly dressed ballplayers wear in the 80s is a far cry from the baggy, bulky uniform of a few decades ago.

To maintain a high fashion image on the diamond, a well-outfitted team needs a private tailor; molding machines and diemakers; imported hides; weavers; specialists in galvanized metal; a wide range of plastics, nylon, twills, polyesters, satins and rubber compositions; and uniform designers, logo-creators and embroiderers.

In fact, it takes over two dozen manufacturers to make the local heroes look sharper than the bums on the opposing team. Club owners want a sleek, colorful, stylish, sales-oriented appearance for their athletes, and are willing to pay about $1300 per player per season to get it, according to big-league equipment managers. That price includes all-new jerseys, pants, shoes, undershirts and a variety of field jackets, which are replaced every single season of a player's career.

In earlier days, the New York Yankees in their svelte pinstripes were considered the epitome of elegance. Today, a dozen teams can lay claim to being the best-dressed, among them the St. Louis Cardinals, Baltimore Orioles, Los Angeles Dodgers, Kansas City Royals and Pittsburgh Pirates.

After a light rubdown from the trainer, wearing nothing but clogs, the player sits in a chair near his 4' × 4' locker and first pulls on cotton **jockey shorts**. Over that goes a **jockstrap** with aluminum cup. Cost: $8.50. Next comes a T-shirt with woolen sleeves and nylon body, and on top of this an **undershirt**

or **sweatshirt**—either sleeveless or, in cold weather, with full-length sleeves. On hot days, pitchers make up to four changes of sweat-drenched shirts between innings. Cost for a set of 6 shirts of the two types: $97.25.

Any needed taping is done now—ankles, knees, sore feet or thighs. Baseball uses a light, rubberized adhesive bandage rather than the heavier tape used in football.

Following this, a player slips on his *sanitaries,* or cotton sweat socks. These reach to the bottom of the knee and fold over. They're white so that in event of a

bleeding cut, no coloring compound can infect the injury (men who are embarassed by skinny legs sometimes pile on 3 pair of socks as a disguise). Over these go the traditional **stirrup stockings,** which run under the feet and up either side of the leg. An elastic band or tape holds both *sannies* and stirrups in place. Some players wear their contrasting-color stirrups a high and flashy 12-14″ above their shoetops in defiance of a rule stating that all players' socks "must be of uniform trim and style." Cost: $7 per set.

Now the player dons his **uniform trousers** and **jersey**. The cut and fabric of *unies* has changed vastly since World War II, from figure-hiding floppy bloomers and roomy shirts of wool flannel to skin-huggers of doubleknit nylon-polyester. "Unies stretch all 4 ways," says Dodger equipment boss **Nobe Kawana**. "That enables them to be cut very tight and streamlined." Suits are custom-fit by manufacturers' tailors. Each spring, tailors

True of false? **Ty Cobb** *and* **Stan Musial** *pitched in the major leagues. It's true — but Musial pitched to just one batter (as a publicity stunt) and Cobb threw only a few games.*

descend upon training camps and measure each man for size and body peculiarities. They then make up 4 sets of uniforms: 2 home-game *whites* and 2 road-trip *greys* (often silver-grey). Most shirts are V-neck pullovers with set-in sleeves and saddle shoulders, though some teams still use the old-fashioned button-front jersey. Pants are very flexible despite their tightness.

Onetime New York Yankee pitching great **Lefty Gomez** says, "Compared to what **Ted Williams** and **Stan Musial** wore, uniforms of the 1980s are like Cadillacs to Model-T Fords. These outfits are bathing suits alongside the old floppers we wore." The cost of the modern uniform: $110 for one set—$440 total.

Shirt emblems, or logos, have become highly creative. Team names are displayed in type styles ranging from Old English to script to modern block letters, or sometimes in crests with the team's initials, on the jersey's front along with the player's number. Player names appear on the shirt's back or in a name-number combination. Decorations are a blatant appeal to the fans' civic pride, ranging from the St. Louis Cardinals' cocky little birds perched on a bat to the California Angels' gold halo and outline of the home state; from the Cleveland Indians' **Chief Wahoo** emblem to the Houston Astros' star of Texas and shoulder stripes—although the Yankee insignia, a red, white and blue top hat and bat superimposed on a red-ringed baseball, is perhaps the most envied. Sleeve logos, piping, colored and paneled caps and bright waistbands add to the dazzling look.

The simple, streamlined, comfortable nature of the baseball uniform has made certain parts of it popular with non-players as well. Baseball-style caps, for example, are made in every color imaginable, trimmed with everything from business logos to off-color messages, and worn in countries around the world by people who have never been inside a ballpark. Long-sleeved jerseys are re-created in cotton knit and worn as an alternative to T-shirts. The satin warm-up jackets have become an American fashion classic. But the trend probably started with baseball fans, who spend hundreds of thousands of dollars each year on clothing that bears the official endorsement and colors of their favorite major league teams.

NEW YORK, Oct. 7, 1894 — *The Giants-Baltimore Orioles game was replete with incidents.*

The discordant notes from the fish horns among the crowd of 20,000 caused a stampede in the horse shed. One animal upset his carriage, broke the harness and raced about the field in panic. He stopped the game, but finally was captured in left field.

One of the side rails of the free seats collapsed and a dozen persons fell to the ground. Bodies were evacuated.

While a band played 'Carry The News To Mary,' Umpire Tim Hurst was knocked unconscious by a foul tip.

Another fight between John McGraw of the Orioles and Umpire Emslie had to be broken up before they spoiled each other's appearance.

(Otherwise it was a calm day at Giants Park, with the home team beating Baltimore 4-1)

Roly-poly **Babe Ruth** *was the reason the New York Yankees adopted their handsome trademark pinstriped uniform. When Ruth ballooned from 215 lbs in 1923 to 260 in 1925, Yankee owner* **Jake Ruppert** *observed, "He looks like a load of hay out there." His chest measured 45", but his waist was almost 50". Wearing thin pinstripes somewhat slenderized the Bambino. To this day, the Yanks stick to the pin pattern on white jersey and trousers.*

Honus Wagner *was the first player ever to endorse a baseball bat.*

Catchers are the most expensively attired of all. They're loaded with:

1 *Triple-bar wire* **mask** with throat protector flap attachment ($30)

Baseball shoes come in four main types. The accent is on lightness, not durability.

For **infielders** and **outfielders,** tops are made of cowhide or kangaroo hide. Soles are plastic. When the sole is molded in the factory, while it is still soft, galvanized steel spikes or **cleats** are embedded. The 3/8″ ground-grippers are arranged with one spike at the toe and 2 more set back 3″ on either side. Three are placed in the heel in a triangular pattern. The 6-cleat arrangement is best for players at positions demanding stability for lightning starts in any direction. The shoes cost about $75 per pair.

Shoes for fields with synthetic surfaces are cleatless. They come instead with 150 or more little vulcanized rubber nubs which supply better traction on Astroturf, Super Turf or Tartan Turf, and they cost around $52.

All-nylon footgear is preferred by about half the players because it is lightweight—a pair weighs only 14-17 oz. These are sprinter's-type shoes from the factories of Adidas, Puma, Nike and other international producers of world-class track-and-field gear. Cost: $55.

Pitcher's footwear is similar to that of other fielders, but with a thickly built-up plastic toe. This hard, bulbous affair prevents the shoe from wearing out quickly where the pitcher plants his foot against the rubber as he powers into his delivery. Cost: $85.

For many years, all-black shoes were the pro standard, but now they come in uniform-complementing white, red, blue, green—and any other color a team could want—all decorated with the single and triple sidestripes or curved stripes that are the trademarks of the various manufacturers. All-Star-caliber players, in return for wearing a product and endorsing it, get 5 or 6 pairs free. Beyond that, as much as $100,000 may be paid to a superstar for advocating a particular brand.

After donning underwear, socks, uniform and shoes, ballplayers assemble their equipment.

2 Plastic and canvas chestpad ($40)

On a road trip, a traveling squad is backed up by more armament and other equipage than a squad of Army infantrymen—more than 3000 lbs of it, crammed into dozens of duffle bags. Duffs, which have replaced the old-time traveling trunks, measure 14″ × 31″ and cost teams $55 apiece.

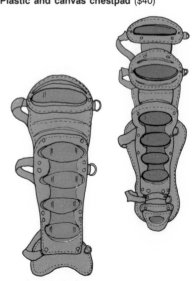

3 Thick **shinguards** of plastic with an extension shielding the toes against wild pitches and foul tips ($60)

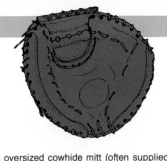

4 An oversized cowhide mitt (often supplied for free by a promotion-conscious maker)

All together, the catcher carries 8½-10 lbs of equipment. A *backstop's* pieces of gear have been called his *tools of ignorance*—for what guy with brains would choose to become a broken-fingered catcher?

At least four kinds of **jackets** and **sweatsuits** are issued:

5 The heavyweight model for chilly weather is of nylon satin with a heavy pile or quilted lining, and costs $80.

6 The medium-weight jacket of stretch nylon is worn in pregame warmups. Cost: $35.

7 Lightweight jackets, or windbreakers, are of nylon taffeta and run about $30.

8 The parka-like, ankle-length, freeze-proof **swaddler** is used in such places as San Francisco's windy, bone-chilling Candlestick Park. The outside is rubberized, with a hood and a heavy pile interior. It costs about $90.

9 Both rubberized and regular sweatsuits are supplied for players who want to lose weight by running.

Caps come in sizes 6½-7¾ and are made of either wool or polyester. Fans snatch away so many as souvenirs that big league clubs need at least 4000 each season. Teams get very creative with caps. The Baltimore Orioles looked snappy on TV while drubbing the Philadelphia Phillies in the 1983 World

Series in their orange-and-black lids with 2 white front panels and an orange-and-black oriole's head centered on the crown. Some clubs sport a higher-than-usual *navy peak* crown (like the scarlet-and-blue cap of the Minnesota Twins). Caps cost about $15.

In the dugout, awaiting a turn at bat, players store their protective **helmets** in an open-faced locker. The hard hat is the essential defense against *headhunter* or *beanball* pitchers and was first used by the Brooklyn Dodgers in 1941. Owner **Branch Rickey** grew weary of seeing his players dizzied—or worse, injured—by skull-crunching fastballs. Thinking helmets to be sissy, most players at first refused to wear them. But some near-fatalities made helmets mandatory in the late 1950s. Originally, they were of fiberglass, but this was replaced with a stronger shell of a plastic called *Cycolac*. Modern helmets are molded in a round shape which *sweeps off* or deflects most pitches to the head.

Almost all helmets—which are worn over the regular playing cap—are equipped with an ear flap (or double flaps) guarding the lower part of the head on the side exposed to the pitcher. When **Ron Cey,** then with the Dodgers, was struck in the 1981 World Series, he said, ''My helmet saved my life.'' Popular models come from the American Baseball Cap Co., have a 2-season lifespan and cost about $29 each.

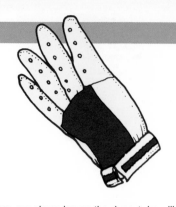

Sliding pads and **elastic knee bandages** are optional items of gear. Six-ounce pads, worn in slots at the rear of the trousers, help cut down abrasions or *strawberries*—although they are no longer seen much in the game. When **Maury Wills** of the Dodgers stole a then-record of 104 bases in 1962, he discarded sliding pads. "They bunch up when sweaty and slow me down," said Wills. So these days, most of the top base thieves don't use the protectors and suffer the cuts instead. But stretch knee guards are common.

Before our player leaves the dugout, he will likely grab 3 more items. A **wristband** of cotton catches perspiration trickling down the arm. **Sunglasses** are worn by outfielders and often, too, by infielders facing into a brilliant sun. Some wear *instant-flip* goggles that are engineered with a spring-loaded mechanism and little levers on each side. Worn under the bill of the cap, the shades can be dropped into or out of place with a flick of a finger. Price: $11. **Batting gloves,** adopted from golf, are made with colorful nylon panels. They are usually worn on both hands, and some men wear a batting glove inside their fielding glove. Cost: $16 a pair.

Over a scorching season, many players also require a **sunscreen ointment** on their faces. To cut down glare, **grease** or **lampblack** may be applied below the eyes.

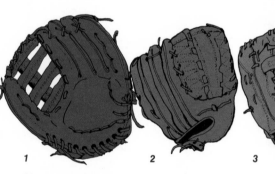

1 2 3 4

Gloves and **mitts** are masterpieces of the leathermaker's craft. Before the 1920s, handgear was skimpy and unpadded and had almost no shock-absorbing quality. In 1918, **Bill Doak** of the Cards invented a cushioned glove with a built-up heel to form a V-shaped pocket, and more sophisticated designs followed quickly. Today's U-shaped fielder's glove, with multiple laces, webbing between the fingers and thumb and a deep ball-swallowing pocket has changed the game greatly by vastly reducing the number of errors.

Baseball rule 1.13 limits fielder's gloves, other than those worn by the first baseman and catcher, to 12″ in length from top to bottom and 8″ in width from thumb crotch to outer edge. The **first baseman's glove** is a *scoop,* measuring a huge 13½-14″ from heel to top. Wilson's popular A-2802 model has webbing for extra thickness between the fingers and thumb, 19 holes for the rawhide lacing and is a veritable trap for either ground or fly balls. A first baseman standing 6′2″ can reach almost 8′ high when stretching for a throw—without leaving the ground.

1 **Infielder's gloves** with 4 separate fingers and thumb are a relatively stubby 9¼″ from heel to tip. They are designed to be worn

loosely on a shortstop, 2nd or 3rd baseman's hand. A loop of leather built into the interior frees the fielders from thrusting hands deeply into the glove, while still maintaining a secure hold and maximum pocket action.

2 **Pitchers' gloves** are 13″, with finger and thumb sections connected by a checkerboard weave of thick leather (to conceal their grips from the batter).

3 **Outfielders' gloves** are similar to those of pitchers—flexible *butterfly nets.*

4 **Catcher's mitts** once were big pillows, running to 45″ in circumference. But a 1965 rule limits pads to 38″ in circumference and 15½″ from top to bottom. With a knuckle-baller on the mound who deals up crazily-breaking balls, catchers switch to a lighter, more pliable mitt called a *snapper.*

If players paid for gloves, they'd be out $50 to $75 per item. However, sporting goods houses from the U.S. to Japan are happy to furnish them with 6 or more models per season. **Reggie Jackson,** power hitter of the California Angels, keeps 8 gloves in reserve. Many players lightly rub vegetable oil into their *heart of the hide* gloves to preserve them and keep them soft.

Bats

Fans watch their idols swinging cudgels of every kind: wide-grain, tight-grain, slim and thick-handled, heavy or small-barreled, solid tan, yellow, black, two-toned, banded, big and small-knobbed, end-cupped or non-cupped. And they wonder: why so much variance? What makes a favorite bat?

"To each his own," explains Philadelphia's **Mike Schmidt,** who averages over 30 home runs per season. "First comes the feel of the stick in your hands. Then it's how that makes you feel mentally." Nothing in baseball is more personal than a player's bat. For Schmidt, the single perfect model doesn't exist; he changes the weight of his bats against fastball, sinkerball, knuckleball and other kinds of pitchers.

But generally, a rather long, whippy *Louisville Slugger* 36″ long and weighing 33 oz suits the needs of this 6'2″ 205-pounder. At 6′ and 182 lbs, smaller **Rod Carew,** 7-time American League hitting champion, favors the lightest bats: 35′ long and only 30 oz. Carew's *broomsticks* helped the California Angel become the modern master of *spray* hitting, slashing balls through the infield for singles.

Depending on height, a ballplayer may use anything from the 37″ *telephone pole* used by the Cincinnati Reds' **Dave Parker** to 5'10″ 190-lb San Diego Padre **Steve Garvey's** 35″ 35 oz club. Whatever the preference, today's bats have a few things in common:

They are constructed of **northern white ash timber** between 40-50 years old.

Bats can be **no more than 2¾″ in diameter** nor **longer than 42″.** No substance may be used on or within them which "improves the distance factor or causes an unusual reaction of the baseball."

Every stick has a **sweet spot**—a place where swingers seek to make contact with the ball. This begins 7-8″ from the tip and is 3-4″ in length. Players precisely determine these few inches by dangling a bat by the knob, tapping it with another bat from the barrel's end down past the trademark, and listening. When a strongly solid sound is heard, that's the sweet spot.

Today's bats are **much lighter** than the hefty-handled, big-nosed 36-43 oz bats used by **Lou Gehrig, Babe Ruth, and Jimmy Foxx** in the 1920s and '30s: average weight now is a mere 32-33 oz. Handles are a skinny 3¾″ in circumference, which is a main reason why 2 or 3 bats are usually broken per game—up to 500 per team each season. In the long ball era, it's believed that a slim bat arched with great arm and hand speed produces more extra-base hits.

Most big leaguers are supplied by makers with name-stamped custom bats. Stars often visit such leading mills as **Hillerich & Bradsby** and **Adirondack** to select a particular wood and grain for autographing. H&B alone has more than 300 different models designed for major league use.

Manufacture Strong hickory was once used, but long ago it was replaced by springier, lighter white ash. Most of the wood comes from the Adirondack and Catskill ranges of New York and northern Pennsylvania. Only second-growth trees are used. After a half century, they're ready to be cut, and each tree will supply enough wood for 60 bats.

After months of air-drying, *billets* of rounded wood are cut to even lengths of 37″, sorted and weighed. From this *rough-out* form, they're shaped into bats on lathes. Calipers give exact tapering and balancing. Numerous finishes are applied: clear lacquer or *natural,* dark barrel with natural handle or *Walker,* and many others. **George Brett,** the Kansas City Royals' walloper, prefers no finish whatsoever. **Bill Madlock,** Pirates, and **Reggie Jackson,** Angels, demand an all-black finish. Others want flame-treated wood.

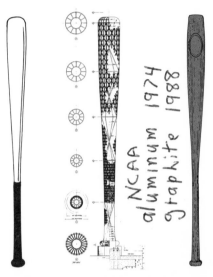

1) Aluminum bat. 2) Batcolumn *sculpture by artist Claes Oldenburg, located in Chicago's Social Security Administration Building. 3) Wooden bat. The oval-shaped spot on the barrel is the* sweet spot; *note how the bat's shape differs from the aluminum version.*

To save weight, some sluggers have their sticks factory-cupped (hollowed out 2″ or more at the barrel end). **Pete Rose,** Expos, says he saves 1½ oz by cupping, which trims this veteran's bats down to 32 oz. Rose, among others, wipes his sticks with alcohol before every game. Smudges left by the ball tell him whether he's swinging late or too early. Use of adhesive pine tar, rubbed onto the handle for a tighter grip, is legal from the grip up to 18″ from the knob's tip. A *Tar Wars* brouhaha broke out in 1983 when George Brett was deprived of a home run when his use of sticky stuff was ruled excessive; it took American League president **Lee McPhail** to finally resolve that the home run was legal.

Cost Twenty years ago, teams paid $3.98 per bat, but that's been inflated today to $12. Since each man owns 3 dozen or more sticks, teams buy up to 2500 each season at a cost of $30,000 or more. **Brooks Robinson,** legendary Baltimore third baseman, had 300 bats in his collection.

Broken bats The number of broken and chipped bats has grown astronomically as pitchers become taller and more powerful (they now often throw 87-93 mph fastballs). Flamethrower **Chris Short,** Phillies, once shattered 9 Dodger bats in one game.

The strangest broken bat incident of all time may have happened in the minors' Texas League in 1952. Houston player **Bud Hardin's** bat split in two when he hit a bouncer to 3rd base. The largest part flew toward 3rd as the baseman prepared to field the ball. Just then the bat piece hit the ball, *again*—knocking it into the stands! Ruling: Hardin was out for striking the ball twice.

Other bat types Before stepping to the plate, a player will warm up with 1 or 2 heavy lead *doughnuts* slipped over the bat to make it feel much lighter when the metal is removed. Aluminum bats used by school teams and junior leagues are chipless and almost breakproof, but big leaguers remain prejudiced against *laboratory stuff,* saying that balls rocket too fast off aluminum. Also, metal gives off a *ping* sound at contact, rather than a nice, loud **c—rrack!** Fungo bats are extra-long, slim bats used by coaches to hit fly balls to fielders in practice. They produce tremendous loft. Some have a shaved flat face and the accuracy to drop a ball inches from the glove of a flycatcher.

Bases

If you've ever wondered what prevents bases from ripping loose under the constant impact of runners' spikes, the answer lies buried in the soil beneath each of the 3 sacks: A 10″ × 10″ concrete block weighing 25 lbs. An anchor stake 8″ long rises through the block to 1″ below the ground. Over the stake fits a thick anchor body. This in turn is fastened to a flat anchor plate which is 4-bolted to the base's bottom. It makes for a rigid, immobile assembly.

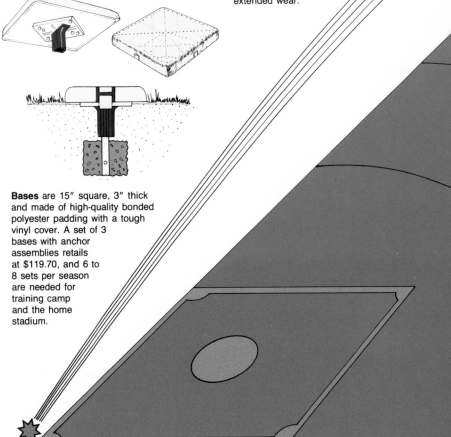

Bases are 15″ square, 3″ thick and made of high-quality bonded polyester padding with a tough vinyl cover. A set of 3 bases with anchor assemblies retails at $119.70, and 6 to 8 sets per season are needed for training camp and the home stadium.

Home plate is a flush-to-the-ground slab so heavy—20 lbs—that no anchoring is needed under it. It's one piece of molded vinyl 4″ thick, with beveled edges to prevent players' shoe spikes from catching on it. Outlining the plate for the pitcher's benefit is a black apron forming a stripe 1½″ wide. Moundsmen call balls thrown to fly over some part of the apron *pitching the black;* usually, umpires refer to them as *strikes.*

Home plates are 5-sided. The flat front faces the pitcher and the sharp tip points toward the catcher at the rear. The point is a 90° angle, fitting it into the junction of the foul lines at the plate. It's 17″ wide and 23″ from front to rear. Cost is $42.30 per platter, and at least 7 are required per ball park—4 for the 2 bullpens, 2 for pre-game warmups, and 1 for the field itself.

The **pitcher's plate** or *rubber* is 24″ long with 4 sides, each 6″ wide. The plate is hollow inside, and reinforced with aluminum tubing. The 4 sides may be rotated to the surface position for extended wear.

The longest major league game played all on one day went into the books on 1 May 1920 at Boston Braves field.

The Brooklyn Dodgers couldn't push a run across for 21 straight innings; the Braves had no results for 20 straight frames. Ultimately, 26 innings were played, and the game ended with a 1-1 tie:

Brooklyn: 0 0 0 0 0 1 0 0 0 0 0 0 0 0 0 0 0 0 0 0 0 0 0 0 0 0—1
Boston: 0 0 0 0 0 1 0 0 0 0 0 0 0 0 0 0 0 0 0 0 0 0 0 0 0 0—1

Most amazing of all, the 2 starting pitchers, **Leon Cadore** of the Dodgers and **Joe Oeschger** of the Braves, went the whole distance! After throwing nearly the equivalent of 3 full games in 1 day, both spent several days in bed.

Major league elapsed-time record for a single game: 23 innings in 7 hrs 23 min—San Francisco vs. New York; 31 May 1964 (final score 8-6, Giants)

Most runs scored in a major league game: 49 runs—Chicago Cubs 26, Philadelphia Phillies 23; 25 August 1922

Longest major league night game: 25 innings—St. Louis Cardinals vs. New York Mets; 11 September 1974 (final score 4-3, Cards)

Most players used in 1 major league game: 51 players in 15 innings—Oakland A's 30, Chicago White Sox 21; 19 September 1972 (final score 8-7, Sox)

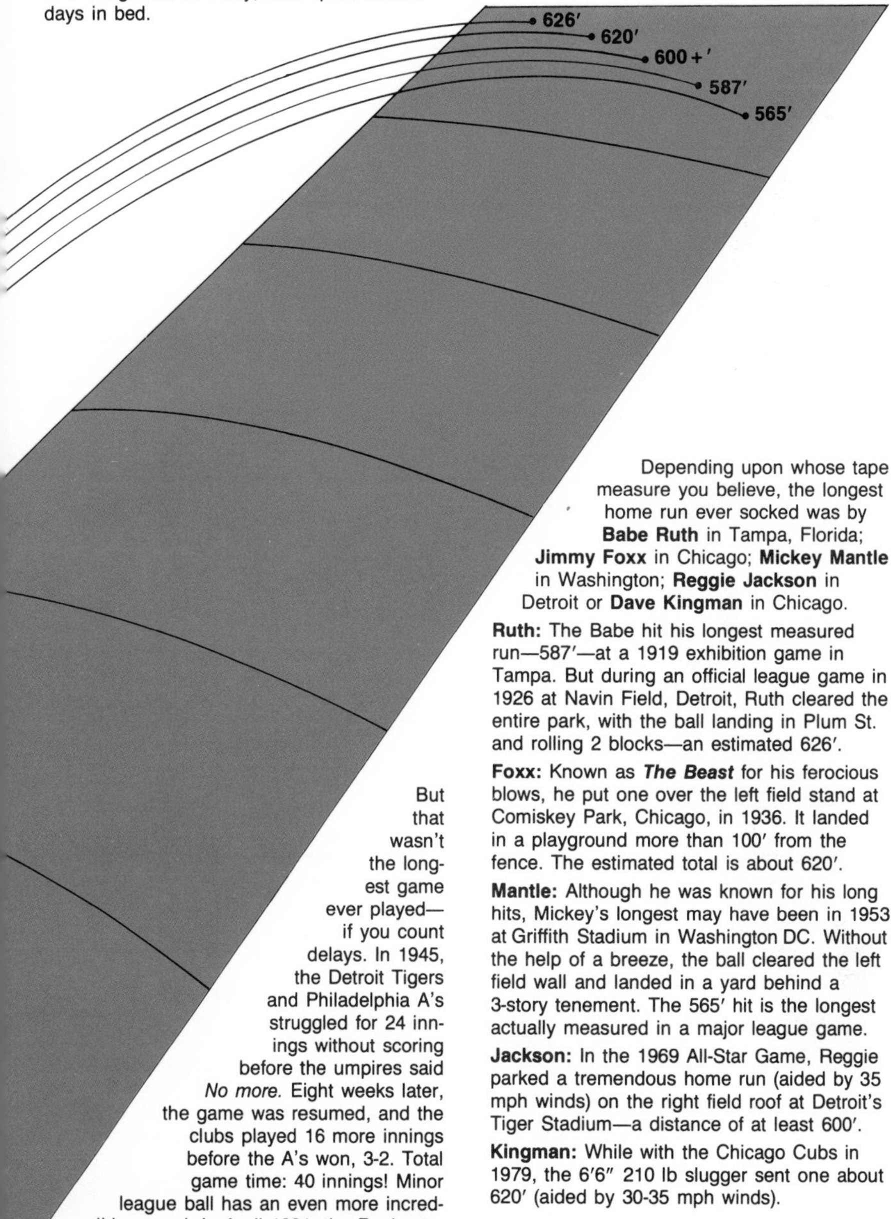

626'
620'
600 + '
587'
565'

But that wasn't the longest game ever played—if you count delays. In 1945, the Detroit Tigers and Philadelphia A's struggled for 24 innings without scoring before the umpires said *No more.* Eight weeks later, the game was resumed, and the clubs played 16 more innings before the A's won, 3-2. Total game time: 40 innings! Minor league ball has an even more incredible record. In April 1981, the Rochester Red Wings and Pawtucket Red Sox began a game on Saturday and finished on Sunday, when Pawtucket scored 1 run in the 33rd inning to win, 3-2. There were 213 at-bats, 59 strikeouts and 156 balls used.

Depending upon whose tape measure you believe, the longest home run ever socked was by **Babe Ruth** in Tampa, Florida; **Jimmy Foxx** in Chicago; **Mickey Mantle** in Washington; **Reggie Jackson** in Detroit or **Dave Kingman** in Chicago.

Ruth: The Babe hit his longest measured run—587'—at a 1919 exhibition game in Tampa. But during an official league game in 1926 at Navin Field, Detroit, Ruth cleared the entire park, with the ball landing in Plum St. and rolling 2 blocks—an estimated 626'.

Foxx: Known as *The Beast* for his ferocious blows, he put one over the left field stand at Comiskey Park, Chicago, in 1936. It landed in a playground more than 100' from the fence. The estimated total is about 620'.

Mantle: Although he was known for his long hits, Mickey's longest may have been in 1953 at Griffith Stadium in Washington DC. Without the help of a breeze, the ball cleared the left field wall and landed in a yard behind a 3-story tenement. The 565' hit is the longest actually measured in a major league game.

Jackson: In the 1969 All-Star Game, Reggie parked a tremendous home run (aided by 35 mph winds) on the right field roof at Detroit's Tiger Stadium—a distance of at least 600'.

Kingman: While with the Chicago Cubs in 1979, the 6'6" 210 lb slugger sent one about 620' (aided by 30-35 mph winds).

The earliest no-hitter pitched in any pro baseball season was thrown by the Detroit Tigers' **Jack Morris** *on 7 April 1984—just 4 days after the season began.*

Perhaps one of the reasons baseball enjoys worldwide popularity is that people of all sizes—not just the very muscular or extra tall—can play it well.

Yet a new generation of major league players is changing the egalitarian nature of the sport: Of 1983's 14 top rookies, 10 of them stood 6'3" or more and averaged close to 200 lbs. And some of them hadn't even reached their full size yet!

Among them—typical of a breed of giants threatening to dominate the game—were 6'6" Rookie of the Year **Darryl Strawberry,** New York Mets outfielder; 6'8" **Mike Smithson,** Texas Rangers pitcher; and 6'5" **Craig McMurtry,** Atlanta Braves pitcher. "The 7' ballplayer is just around the corner, I'd guess," says veteran A's infielder **Joe Morgan.** At 5'7" and 160 lbs, Morgan feels dwarfed. He's one of the few smaller men surviving in the majors.

There have always been big players the likes of **Boog Powell** of Baltimore, **Frank Howard** of the Dodgers, **Willie McCovey** of San Francisco and **Hank Greenberg** of Detroit—but these 6'4" and 6'7" men would be ordinary nowadays. Managers and scouts once looked for players who had speed, strong throwing arms and quick reflexes; height and bulk were secondary assets. But now big brutes are wanted up and down the lineup, even in the middle infield, which was traditionally the territory of 150-pounders.

Pitchers Nowhere is the new demand for size more evident than on the mound. On major league rosters during the 1983 season no fewer than 169 flingers stood 6'3" or more. The Cincinnati Reds hurling corps had 2 men at 6'6", 2 at 6'5" and 4 who were 6'4". Even taller were the California Angels, with 9 pitchers topping 6'4" and a pair at 6'7". **Fred Lynn,** an Angels outfielder of relatively modest dimensions (6'1" 188 lbs), says, "I'm awed by the size of modern pitchers. We hitters are facing monsters weighing 230 lbs, with arms long as a pro basketballer's. They throw rockets."

Infielders The defensive spots once filled by such diminutive greats as **Phil Rizzuto, Luis Aparicio** and **Nellie Fox** are now occupied by players with a combination of size and muscle. No longer is the 1st baseman the infield's only heavyweight: In the '83 World Series, the winning Baltimore Orioles had 6'4" **Cal Ripken** at shortstop and 6'1" **Rich Dauer** at 2nd base. First baseman **Eddie Murray,** 6'2" and 200 lbs, and 6' 3rd baseman **Todd Cruz** completed the infield. A 3rd baseman such as powerful 6'3" **Nick Esasky** of Cincinnati isn't a curiosity, just a big man able to play a position calling for extreme agility. But 1st basemen, such as 6'4" **Kent Hrbek** (Minnesota) and **Cliff Johnson** (Toronto) still grow ever bigger.

Outfielders Comparatively, **Willie Mays** (5'10", 175 lbs), **Mickey Mantle** (5'10" 190 lbs) and **Stan Musial** (6' 175 lbs)—three of the all-time best—would look short beside current flychasers. Scouts look for fielders who mix swiftness with plate power, such as Atlanta's 6'5" **Dale Murphy,** the Phillies' 6'6"

Von Hayes, the Dodgers' 6'5" **Mike Marshall** and the Montreal Expos' 6'4" **Andre Dawson.** Joe DiMaggio remarks wryly, "We used to think, on the Yankees of the 1940s, that **Charlie** *King Kong* **Keller** at 210 lbs was a helluva hunk of a guy. Now they've got bat boys weighing that much."

In the face of all this it seems miraculous that, as late as 1980, 5'5½" **Freddie Patek** (California Angels) could still find a place on the field, or that 5'8½" **Davey Lopes** could star with the Dodgers. Although few smaller players are left, their tribe includes such solid performers as 5'8" 185 lb **Ron Cey** of the Chicago Cubs, 5'8" **Glenn Hubbard** of the Atlanta Braves and 5'6" **Onix Conception** of Kansas City.

These men are reminders that the small—but never meek—almost have inherited the baseball earth at various times. While the giants already dominate other pro sports and are moving in on baseball, the fact remains that a man measuring 5'4¼" registered one of the 10 highest batting averages in baseball history. A 5'6" player was once the American League MVP. And a 5'7" 155-pounder once led the NL in slugging percentage.

Among the diminutive dynamos who left their mark on the game:

William *Wee Willie* **Keeler** He called himself the "rum hound and champion drinker" of baseball—yet Keeler batted as high as .432 in the 1890s, played until 1910 and averaged .345 lifetime. His specialty was to "hit 'em where they ain't." Size: 5'4½", 135 lbs.

Walter *Rabbit* **Maranville** The Boston Nationals' star lasted 23 tough NL years—still the league record for longevity. Size: 5'6", 155 lbs.

Stanley *Bucky* **Harris** Between 1919 and 1931, he played 2nd base for Washington and Detroit—and it couldn't have been better covered if he'd thrown a blanket over it. In 1924, the 28-year-old manager-player led the Washington Senators to a World Series triumph over **John McGraw's** Giants. Size: 5'7", 156 lbs.

Phil *Scooter* **Rizzuto** The AL's Most Valuable Player in 1950, when he hit .324, Scooter led the league in fielding and was an inspiration for the New York Yankees. He had 15 seasons with the Yanks, setting an AL record for most games—289—without an error. Size: 5'6", 145 lbs.

Albert *Little Albie* **Pearson** Pearson led the California Angels in hitting. With the smallest strike zone ever seen—13"—he relaxed in the outfield (it was said) by leaning against a blade of grass, and was the best lead-off hitter in the major league during the early 1960s. Size: not quite 5'5", 144 lbs.

Joe *Little Joe* **Morgan** He began playing big league ball back in 1964, and he's still going strong with the Oakland A's. Morgan was the first man to steal 60 bases *and* hit 25 or more homers in 1 season—he once made 6 hits in one game. Named NL MVP in 1975-76. Size: 5'7", 145 lbs.

Freddie Patek Performing for the California Angels in the 1980s and a longtime Kansas City Royals star before that, Patek is the 1890s Wee Willie Keeler reincarnated. Like Keeler, Patek carries a powerful sting. He led AL shortstops in making double plays for 4 seasons, and once hit 3 home runs in one game. Size: 5'5", 148 lbs.

AGES

Leroy *Satchel* Paige began his unparalleled career with the Birmingham Black Barons in 1926. In 1965, he pitched his final game—for the Kansas City A's.

Only a few moundsmen have lasted for 20 years; only one played for almost 40, and that was Satch Paige—perhaps the greatest flinger who ever lived.

Here are the longevity records of the game's grand old men:

All-time oldest player **Leroy Paige,** age 60 years, 2 months, 18 days

Oldest rookie Paige, age 42 when the Cleveland Indians finally gave him his first shot in the white major leagues

Oldest batting leader **Ted Williams** led with a .328 average in 1958 at the age of 40

Oldest home run leader **Babe Ruth** was 36 when he hit 46 home runs to tie with **Lou Gehrig** for the AL title in 1931

Most years played in majors **Eddie Collins** played second base and shortstop for 25 years between 1906-1930

Most years pitched in majors **Early Wynn** (1939-63) and **John *Jack* Quinn** (1909-1933) both pitched 23 years

Most years catching **Bob O'Farrell,** 21 years (1915-35)

Most years at 1st base **Willie McCovey,** 22 years (1959-80)

Most years at 2nd base **Eddie Collins,** 21 years (1908-28)

Most years at 3rd base **Brooks Robinson,** 23 years (1955-77)

Most World Series participations **Lawrence *Yogi* Berra,** 14 appearances between 1947-63

Youth has been represented, too, with some remarkably precocious kids breaking into the big league lineups:

All-time youngest players In the NL, **Joe H. Nuxhall** pitched for Cincinnati at 15 years, 316 days; in the AL, **Carl A. Scheib** began pitching for Philadelphia at 16 years, 248 days

Youngest batting leader In 1955, Detroit outfielder **Al Kaline** hit .340 to lead the AL at the age of 20 years, 280 days; in 1941 Brooklyn infielder/outfielder **Harold *Pete* Reiser** led the NL with a .343 average at age 22 years, 114 days

ANNOUNCERS

In 1913, someone hooked a microphone to the home plate umpire's mask at New York's Polo Grounds, and baseball announcing was born.

"Now batting, **Lefty O'Doul**," the ump bawled, and gave the ball and strike count to the Giants crowd as the game progressed. Not long after that experiment, radio began to emerge in a regional, tentative way. In 1921 the country's first radio station, KDKA in Pittsburgh, broadcast the first ball game; by 1923 New York's WEAF had put mellow-voiced **Graham McNamee** behind the mike, making him the first widely known sports announcer. The game had a hard time lining up sponsors for radiocasts at first. It wasn't until 1934 that a big event like the World Series could be sold: auto tycoon **Henry Ford** paid $400,000 for 4 years of Series games in the first sponsorship deal.

The public came to love radio accounts, whether they were live or recreations of games in distant towns announced by a local broadcaster who worked off a teletype machine. In Chicago, a young sportscaster named *Dutch* **Reagan** became popular for his imaginative descriptions and self-made sound effects; the story is told that one day the teletype broke down momentarily and he announced imaginary foul balls until it was working again.

No other baseball *voice* became US president, but today the telecasters and radio announcers are in many cases as famous—and well-paid—as the athletes on the diamond.

TV cameras first focused on baseball on 26 August 1939 at Brooklyn's Ebbets Field. **Walter *Red* Barber** did the talking for NBC; in the first show Cincinnati pitcher **Bucky Walters** created a sensation when he demonstrated how he gripped his curveball.

Today, rooters in every city identify with their home-town sportscasters. Among the favorites are **Ernie Harwell** of WJR in Detroit; **Vin Scully,** who has been with the Dodgers since they were in Brooklyn; **Bob Prince,** who calls Pirates games in Pittsburgh; and **Bill King** and **Lon Simmons,** who work as a team covering the Oakland A's.

RETIREMENT

For some players, the game doesn't end when the elasticity goes, the legs grow leaden with age and the eyes can no longer follow the darting ball.

Many find a spot somewhere in the game's off-the-field fringes where they can remain close to the action and play out their years in contentment. Among the places that retired baseball players show up:

The front office Such illuminaries as **Stan Musial** and **Joe DiMaggio** sit on the boards of directors of major league teams; **Bobby Avila** is president of the Mexican League; others, like **Hank Aaron, Dallas Green** and **Al Rosen,** serve as general managers.

Public relations, promotion & community services **Bob Feller, Don Newcombe** and **Roy Campanella** have all found niches here.

Scouting Among the bird dogs that began their careers as players are **Whitey Ford, Hank Bauer** and **Eddie Lopat.**

Coaching **Bob Gibson, Red Schoendienst, Ozzie Virgil, Johnny Podres** and **Yogi Berra** are only a few of the game's masters who went on to teach others.

Endorsements Now pitching products are **Jim Palmer, Joe DiMaggio, Boog Powell, Billy Martin, Frank Robinson**...and the Miller Brewing Company's cast of thousands.

Announcing Manning the mike today are **Don Drysdale, Ralph Kiner, Phil Rizzuto, Joe Garagiola, Brooks Robinson** and **Tony Kubek,** among many others.

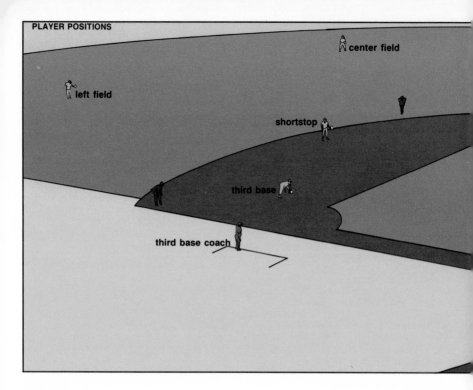

center field

left field

shortstop

third base

third base coach

Mostly, a bench boss sits on the plank and plots, directs, and worries.

But his job becomes pure joy if his team includes these winners:

A pitcher who can sprint 65′ from the mound to beat the batter running down the base line on a ball hit to the 1st baseman and make the out. Many pitchers are too slow to make the play consistently. Equally valuable is the ability to deliver every pitch—fastball, change-of-pace or breaking ball—with an identical motion. Only the greatest hurlers have a uniform delivery that masks their intent.

A catcher with the rare ability to handle a dancing knuckleball (such as **Bruce Benedict** of the Atlanta Braves, a specialist at it), and who can cover home plate on close plays (LA's **Mike Scioscia** does it best).

A lefthanded 1st baseman who's also tall—or fairly so. Southpaw 1st basemen have an edge on righthanders in making the throw to 2nd base after fielding a grounder, since they need not pivot. Height makes him a better target for other infielders—and he can stretch out farther in receiving throws.

Middle infielders who can pivot at 2nd base and make the double play. Both the shortstop and 2nd baseman need to be slick at gloving the ball at the bag, stepping on the base while in motion, and then dodging the incoming runner while making an accurate throw to 1st base.

A 3rd baseman who can charge a bunt or topped ball with a runner on 1st base and, while going toward home plate, whip the ball across his body to 2nd base for the out—a most uncommon talent.

An outfielder who can throw low and accurately to the cut-off man with runners on the bases. Although one runner may advance from 2nd to 3rd base, a canny infielder on the relay may shoot down another runner for a key out.

A hitter who doesn't always try to pull the pitch down the baselines, but uses the entire field with his bat—one who can adjust his stance and bat action to spray the ball, with many a base hit into the *opposite* field (right field for a right-handed batter, left field for a lefty). A hitter who can bunt well is another asset: if the opposing team's 3rd baseman is playing the hitter deep, a smart batter can lay down a bunt toward 3rd and beat the throw to 1st (a favorite strategy of Padre **Steve Garvey**).

A base-stealer with an Olympic sprinter's instant start. He needn't be terrifically fast, but he knows that most bases are stolen with the *first stride taken.* A valuable runner doesn't forget that if a pitch is low and on the 3rd base side, the catcher will take a split second longer to shift into throwing position than if the pitch is to the plate's right side (and almost all catchers are right-handed).

A #8 hitter, batting far down the lineup, who may hit weakly but can get on base regularly with scratch hits, base-on-balls, or the like. Then the 9th man up, the pitcher (who generally can't hit), can bunt him down to 2nd base. If #8 gets on base, it also removes the onus of the pitcher coming to bat first in the next inning and starting things off with an out.

A smart baserunner who can advance a base on a ball hit to the infield's left side when standing at 1st. Many runners don't know whether or not to take off when the 3rd baseman dives for the ball. If he's caught it, they can be doubled off with a quick throw. Sharp runners watch the umpire at 3rd, who immediately signals *out* or *ball in play,* and react accordingly. Smart runners also watch the outfielder and try to steal an extra base when the fielder takes his time returning the ball to the infield.

Of course, the most sought-after player of all is the guy who averages .380 with 50 home runs per season. Naturally, players like that come along very rarely—but it's the little things that win games.

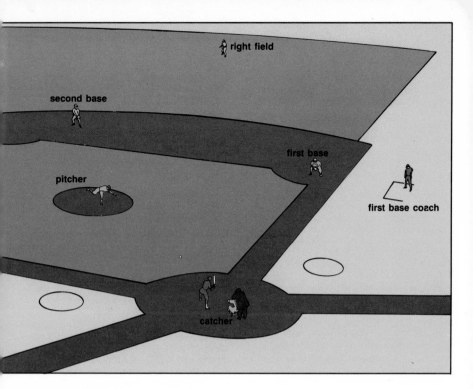

second base

right field

pitcher

first base

first base coach

catcher

What players want most in a manager:
One who won't stoop so low as to bribe a hotel night-shift elevator operator to request an autographed ball from a player coming home at 3 am—as New York Giants manager **John McGraw** once did—to prove that a victim has broken curfew. And one who doesn't panic in a long losing streak and depart from the proven percentage moves to try desperate maneuvers.

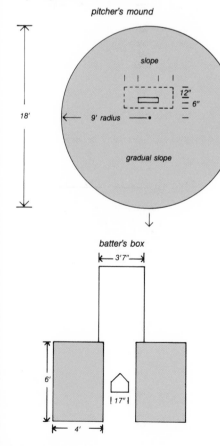

pitcher's mound

slope

12"
6"

18'

9' radius

gradual slope

batter's box

3'7"

6'

17"

4'

Coaches do far more than relay signals: they're specialists in instructing pitchers, hitters or fielders. Four to 6 are employed by a major league club; some chart every opponent's pitch by type, location, repeat tendency and result. Others supervise the bullpen, linked to the manager by telephone. Senior coaches take over when the manager is ejected from the park by an infuriated umpire.

Base coaches In the coaching boxes, which are 20' × 10' chalked rectangles, are:
1st base coach He reminds the runner at 1st of the number of outs and existing offensive opportunities, and warns him of the pitcher's particular pick-off skill. If the 1st baseman sneaks in behind the runner on a pick-off, the coach yells a warning.
3rd base coach He helps a baserunner sprinting from 1st to 3rd or from 2nd to home plate when the runner can't see the ball. Incoming runners are told by signal when a slide is needed, or when they can come into 3rd base standing. Most vital, this coach must decide when to *wave on* an incoming runner who can make it to home plate, and when to hold him up—a split-second decision in many cases.

Pitching coaches specialize in working with pitchers to develop new skills and improve old ones.

Hitting coaches develop players' batting skills and prepare them to meet specific pitchers.

Dugout coaches assist the manager with strategy.

Bullpen coaches supervise relievers and utility players.

Tony Mullane *won 285 games in the Gay 90s—but that's not what made him famous. He pitched both righthanded and lefthanded, one of a very tiny number of hurlers in big-time history who were ambidextrous.*

TERMS

Appeal A team's claim that an opponent violated a rule, or that an umpire erred and should reconsider, or that a second umpire's opinion is needed in a given situation.

Assist Fielder's credit for helping make an out, usually by throwing the ball to a baseman.

Balk Describes a wide variety of illegal moves by the pitcher, including moving shoulders while pitching from a stretch position, beginning a pitch without following through to completion in the stretch position, throwing a pick-off without stepping in the direction of the intended base, making pitching motions without having the ball, and pitching without a catcher. A ball is awarded if the pitcher puts his pitching hand near his mouth while standing on the pitcher's rubber. All runners advance one base when a balk is called.

Batting Average Found by dividing total times at bat into total base hits. Base-on-balls (walk), catcher's interference, hit by pitch, pitcher's balk or sacrifice are not counted as a time at bat. Ty Cobb's lifetime .367 average is the all-time best.

The Book Time-tested tactics and strategy by which teams operate. There's a *book* for almost every conceivable game situation.

Breaking balls Any pitch that isn't straightly thrown: includes *curve, slider* (between fastball and curve), *screwball* (type of reverse-breaking curve) and *knuckleball* (no spin, unpredictable movement).

Checked Swing Swing of the bat is not completed; the plate umpire must decide if the bat came around far enough to indicate a definite intent to swing, or if the batter truly held back. In the latter case, the swing does not count as a strike unless the pitch was in the strike zone.

Cut-off An infielder intercepts an outfielder's throw and speedily relays it to a baseman while the runners are moving.

Cycle The rare occasion when a batter connects for a single, double, triple and home run in 1 game.

Double Steal 2 baserunners stealing bases simultaneously during one play.

Fielder's Choice A fielder who passes up a throw to 1st base on a batted ball and instead retires a preceding runner at another base.

Earned Run Average (ERA) Multiply by 9 the number of earned runs a pitcher has allowed the opposing team; then divide by the number of innings he has pitched. This gives the average number of earned runs given up per 9 innings pitched. An ERA under 3.50 is good; under 3.00 is excellent. In modern times, **Bob Gibson** of the St. Louis Cards holds the single-season (1968) ERA record—an amazing 1.12.

Grand Slam A home run hit with 3 men on base *(bases loaded)*, scoring 4 runs.

Hit-and-Run A play designed to advance base runners from 1st base to 2nd base when the batting team has fewer than 2 outs. As the runner on 1st starts toward 2nd (as if stealing), the batter hits ball through space deserted by 2nd baseman or shortstop, who must defensively cover 2nd base. A highly skilled batter is needed for this play.

In 1885 **George Strief** *of Philadelphia hit 4 triples in a single game.*

Hole Any open space between 2 infielders, but most commonly the area between the shortstop and 3rd baseman through which hits are drilled.

Infield Fly Rule This puzzles many fans. It applies only when a team has fewer than 2 outs and runners on 1st and 2nd base or on 1st, 2nd and 3rd. If the batter lofts a pop up to the infield which the umpire feels can be handily caught, the batter automatically is out. The rule spares the batting team from an easy double play by an infielder deliberately dropping the ball, forcing trapped runners to advance.

Judgment Call Any umpire's ruling which involves judgment alone (strike or ball, foul ball or fair, safe or out) is the final word on the matter. Managers' screams very rarely change a judgment call.

Leads Distance a runner can safely move off a base without getting picked off by the pitcher or catcher. There are *walking, set, leaning* and *delayed-steal* leads in a runner's repertoire.

Losing Pitcher The pitcher who allowed the opponent to score the runs needed to keep its lead and win. If a starting pitcher gives up 1 run and his replacement gives up 6 runs (for a final score of 7-0), the starting pitcher is still credited with the loss.

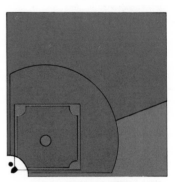

right handed batter

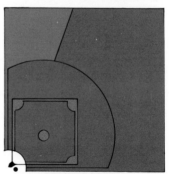

left handed batter

Opposite Field Outfield area away from a batter's natural power. For example, right field is opposite for a right-handed batter, who more naturally hits toward left field (hitting toward left is known as *pulling the ball*).

Pick-off The pitcher whirls, throws to a base (usually 1st) and catches a runner who's strayed too far off the bag—he's out. A pick-off at 2nd base is a pre-arranged, split-timed play, with the 2nd baseman or shortstop breaking from his natural position to cover the bag.

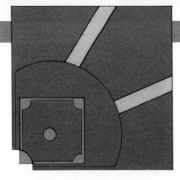

Power Alleys Spaces between outfielders which can't be closed quickly. Double and triples are hit through these slots.

Quick Pitch An illegal delivery following soon after a previous pitch, catching the batter while he is not yet prepared to swing.

Runs-batted-in (RBI) The tally of the number of times a run is scored as direct result of a batter's base hit, base-on-balls, hit-by-pitch, sacrifice fly or ground-out. If the runner scores during a double play, the batter is not credited with an RBI.

Shake-off When the pitcher refuses the type of pitch signaled by the catcher with shake of head or glove.

Signs Offensive or defensive signals given in advance of a play to pass word of the team's intention. Managers signal coaches, who relay the message to players; catchers give pitchers signs; hitters are told when to bunt, *take* (not swing on) a pitch or to hit away. Stealing another club's signs by keen detective work is frowned on, but it's as old as the Old Ball Game.

Slides Many styles are used to slide into bases. The *hook* and *bent-leg* are the most effective. In the first, a leg or toe is hooked around the base with body withdrawn. In the second, one leg is extended to the bag, the other tucked under the body so the player can rise quickly and continue running.

Slugging Average A measure of long-ball hitting ability, arrived at by dividing the total number of bases reached as a result of a single player's hits into his number of times-at-bat. In 1983, Atlanta's **Dale Murphy** averaged .540 and Kansas City's **George Brett** averaged .563, making them the AL and NL slugging leaders. **Babe Ruth's** lifetime .690 average is the all-time record.

Squeeze Play An attempt to score a runner from 3rd base on a bunt. It can be done with the runner waiting until he sees a good bunt made, or he can start his race for home plate just before the pitch is released—a maneuver called a *suicide squeeze,* since it can be fatal if the batter doesn't connect.

Substitution A new player may enter the game at any point, but the man he replaces can't return to the game. The new man takes the spot of the departing individual in the batting order.

Switch hitter A batter who can hit either right or lefthanded. **Mickey Mantle** was a great switcher of the past; **Pete Rose** is today's star.

Tagging Up A complicated rule that goes into effect when a fly ball is caught. Base runners are required to make contact with their starting base (*tag up* with it) *after* the fly is caught before they can proceed to the next one. Usually, a runner leads off to the next base even before the ball is pitched, and may be halfway there before the fly out is caught; the rule forces him to return to his original base and puts him at risk of being trapped between bases. If the runner tags up at 3rd base and then makes a successful try for home plate, the play is known as a *sacrifice fly,* since the batter sacrificed his opportunity to run in order to bring the runner in to score.

Warning track A different-surface track 20' wide or more that encircles the outfield to warn flyhawking fielders that they are nearing the fence.

Wild pitch or *passed ball* A ball pitched obviously beyond a catcher's reach, or bounced on the ground with a runner advancing, is wild. A passed ball describes a catcher's failure to handle a pitch within his normal reach.

Winning Pitcher A starting moundsman who works at least 5 innings of a game, whose team is ahead by 1 or more runs when he is replaced and remains ahead at game's end. Relief pitchers can gain a win credit if, after they come to the mound, their team takes the lead and holds it to the game's conclusion.

Won-lost percentage This is found by dividing a pitcher's number of wins by his total games pitched.

Because he walked with a strut, the New York Giants called him *Turkeylegs* Donlin.

Since he hailed from the backwoods, he was *Hill Billy* **Bildilli** to the St. Louis Browns of the 1930s. Residence in the manager's doghouse gave a Chicago Cubs moundsman the tag of *Fido* **Baldwin.** Two very nervous players were called *Fidgety* **Phil Collins** and *Twitchy Dick* **Porter.** There was *One Arm* **Daly** (although he had only 1 arm, he won 24 games for Cleveland in a single season); a broken-nosed heavy breather named *Wheezer* **Dell,** and a flower lover called *Buttercup* **Dickerson.** In the old days, it seemed like everyone had nicknames:

Sultan of Swat **Babe Ruth** (although teammates called him *Jidge,* a corruption of George, his first name).

Rajah **Hornsby** The obvious tag for **Rogers Hornsby,** the ruling right-handed hitter of all time with a .358 career average.

Georgia Peach **Cobb** A *peach* meant the best in Ty's day and he was all of that.

Iron Horse **Gehrig** A tribute to the Yankee 1st baseman's record: 2130 straight games played over 15 seasons. Also known as *Larrupin Lou.*

Big Six **Mathewson** The 373-game winning hurler of the NY Giants and Cincinnati Reds, Christy was named for a celebrated New York fire engine in 1908. "Certainly Mathewson is the Big Six of pitchers!" said Gotham sportswriter **Sam Crane.**

Grey Eagle **Tris Speaker** played the shallowest outfield, and nothing got by him.

Yankee Clipper **DiMaggio** In full sail, nobody played the outfield like the tall man also known as *Joltin' Joe.*

Stan *The Man* **Musial** His odd corkscrew batting stance gave him a .331 lifetime average.

Say-Hey Kid **Mays** The greeting he gave people became the great Willie's trademark. And it supplanted *Junior,* a name he hated.

Traditionally, sportswriters invented nearly as many tags as players did, but in recent times neither group shows much interest in gilding the lily. These are among the more exotic modern sobriquets:

Mr. October **Reggie Jackson,** California Angels, with 10 home runs in the World Series to date.

Charley Hustle **Pete Rose,** the Expos' perpetual dynamo who outruns everything.

Pops **Willie Stargell,** retired Pittsburgh Pirates' leader with 2 league home run titles.

Goose **Rich Gossage,** the Padre reliever who has thrown over 1000 strikeouts in his career.

Jockstrap Jim **James Alvin Palmer,** Baltimore's 3-time Pitcher of the Year. His near-nude form in underwear ads has earned him many female fans.

The Penguin 5′9″ **Ron Cey's** stubby legs inspired Dodger manager **Tom Lasorda** to invent the nickname.

Tug **Frank Edwin McGraw,** ace Philly reliever, who tugged everything as a kid.

Little Cajun Sometimes used for Louisiana-born **Ron Guidry,** the lefthanded Yankee pitcher and 5′10″ 160-pound whiff specialist.

The Cobra 230-pound **Dave Parker,** the Reds' bomber with swing that strikes out like a snake.

Mr. Bones **Kent Tekulve** of Pittsburgh, a 6′4″ stringbean who unfolds like an activated skeleton with sidearm pitches that kill rallies.

Dave the Rave **Dave Winfield,** Yankee powerhouse hitter with a contract to match.

The Franchise **Tom Seaver,** who won 103 games for the NY Mets in 5 straight seasons, twirling them to 2 pennants and a World Series victory.

Happy That's **Burt Hooton,** the Dodgers' right-handed slider specialist who smiles about as often as the Sphinx.

Doc **George Medich,** the Texas Rangers' pitcher, has professional medical training.

Memorably named managers include: **John *Muggsy* McGraw** (but he punched anyone who called him that); **Cornelius *Connie Mack* McGillicudy** (aka *The Tall Tactician*); **Miller *The Mighty Mite* Huggins,** *Marse Joe* **McCarthy;** *Pongo Joe* **Cantillon;** *Deacon* **Bill McKechnie** and *Uncle* **Wilbert Robinson.** Later on came *Jolly Cholly* **Grimm,** *Bucky* **Harris,** *Shanky* **Farrell,** *Pinky* **Higgins,** *Cookie* **Lavagetto,** *Big Bear* **Hutchinson,** *Casey* **Stengel** and *Smokey* **Alston.**

Clubhouse name-makers can't stand it when players come along with commonplace appellations. They feel compelled to add some color to the lives of Smiths and Joneses:

Jones: Bubber, Nippy, Jumping Jack, Baby, Flip Flap, Available, Midge, Sad Sam

Smith: Broadway, Popboy, Germany, Red, Bull, Pacer

Davis: Coonskin, Kiddo, Stinky, Jumbo, Peaches, Spud, Scat, Brandy

Williams: Gloomy Gus, Mutt, Steamboat, Dib, Kid, Rip, Ace, Pop

---

Strange but true: Pitcher **Dean Stone** *once won a game without ever throwing a single pitch. Stone went to the mound for the AL during the last inning of the 1954 All-Star game, with two men already out. An NL player tried to steal home and Stone threw him out at the plate—making it 3 away.*

And once in a while a new man arrives in the majors with a legal name so terrific that nobody would think of touching it:

Camille Von Brabant
Rachel Slider
Elmer Klumpp
Dimitrihoff Dimitri Ivanovich
Fred Yapp
Moses J. Yellowhorse
Van Lingle Mungo
Ferdinand Maurice Oswals Schupp

Sometimes, an entire team takes a nickname. *The Gas House Gang* of rowdy athletes won NL pennants for the St. Louis Cardinals in 1930-31-34. *Bronx Bombers* has described various Yankee editions. *The Whiz Kids,* Philadelphia's young 1950 NL upset winners, un-whizzed in the World Series, losing in 4 straight to the Yanks. *The Big Red Machine* of Cincinnati captured titles in 1970-72-75-76. And, of course, there were the glorious *Brooklyn Bums* of the 1940s-50s. For blowing the big one, the World Series, nobody had matched the Bums, who lost the classic 4 out of the 5 times they qualified for it between 1949-56, winning only in 1955.

Some confusion exists over how some famous nicknames originated. *Dizzy* **Dean** came not from baseball, but from his earlier Army days when the Arkansas oddball saluted dogfaces and ignored officers. When *Babe* **Ruth** began his career in 1914, his mother was dead and a father he never knew was to die in a bar shooting. **Jack Dunn,** owner of the Baltimore Orioles, took the kid under his wing and Ruth became known as *Jack's Babe.* It stuck. *Old Pete* was Hall of Fame pitcher **Grover Cleveland Alexander,** who fell into a mud-alkali bog as a boy in Texas. Somebody said, ''Well, if it isn't old Alkali Pete, himself,'' and so he was. *Yogi* **Berra** dated to Larry Berra's boyhood in St. Louis, where he liked a movie he saw about a Hindu yogi. *Pee Wee* **Reese** had nothing to do with small size (Harold Henry stood close to 5′10″)—it came from a prize marble he had as a boy.

The game's slang ranges from basic expressions applied through the ages to colorful modern twists.

The batter:
draws (i.e., receives) a base-on-balls
doesn't hit a homerun, but hits a *dinger, tater* or *Vaya,* or *goes downtown*
flares a looping basehit to the close-in outfield or into the stands for a foul
stretches a base hit from a single to a double or more
lays down or *dumps* a bunt
isn't thrown at by the pitcher, but is *dusted* or given the *purpose pitch*
failing to get a game hit, *draws the collar* or *the pipe*
calls home run-prone ballparks *launching pads*
doesn't wear a helmet, but a *hardhat* or *shell*
hits a *nubber* or *squib* (weak ground ball to the infield)
takes a third called strike (no swing), and *goes out looking*

is a *4 o'clock hitter* if he's hot in practice, but a flop under game conditions

hits *ropes, rockets,* or *shots,* not line drives

spoils the pitch by fouling it off

isn't given a base-on-balls, but is *put aboard* or *free ticketed*

gets out in front by anticipating the pitch and swinging too soon

doesn't miss the ball, but *swings through it*

produces a *rally-killer* by hitting into a double play; also *falls through the trapdoor*

hits the ball on the *sweet spot,* gets *good wood* or makes contact *off the trademark*

hits a *Baltimore Chop* (the ball bounds very high in front of plate and over infielders' heads)

if a poor batsman, he *couldn't hit Mollie Poop* or is a *banjo hitter.*

crosses the Mendoza Line when improving his bat average to above .200 (a onetime hitter named **Mario Mendoza** averaged .216 in an 8-year big league career)

The pitcher:

with the catcher, composes a *battery* (a pre-1900 military term for 2 artillery pieces working as a unit)

doesn't throw hard, but *brings it, has hair, comes with The Express* or *throws BBs.*

changes up when throwing with less than usual velocity

wastes one when he deliberately throws a non-strike pitch

works both sides when varying his pitches from right side to left side of the plate

has *good cheese* when his fastball is smoking

if his curves are breaking at their best, is throwing the *yellow hammer, Uncle Charlie* or the *yakker*

is *intellectual* if he has fine control

works from a *stretch* when not fully winding up to throw with runners on base

sends *greeting cards* when he throws on purpose at the batter's head or body

has a *wrinkle* when his curveball is poor

grooves it when throwing a ball over the plate

sets down the side when achieving 3 outs in an inning without yielding a hit

throws *slingshots* or *submarines* if his delivery is underhanded or sidearmed

has an *out* pitch, his favorite delivery and the one he resorts to in retiring a batter (also called a *bread-and-butter pitch)*

drops the arm when his arm grows tired

is a *Century Man* when his fastball is clocked at 100 mph or close to it

has a *positive fastball,* or one that batters are positive they can hit, but can't

Fielders, baserunners:

go airborne in diving for a line drive

don't make a double play, but *turn it*

go *into the hole* to catch a ball hit in the gap between shortstop and 3rd base

play the *initial sack* if they're a 1st baseman, the *keystone bag* if they're a 2nd baseman and the *hot corner* if they're on 3rd

make a pizza of it or *hit metal* when they mess up a ball hit to them

brought their leather to the park when having a stellar fielding day

quit at the wire when running to 1st base and slowing up near the finish; also *dog-trot*

have *angels in the sky,* or clouds which help cut the sun's glare on a flyball

have a *strong gun* as a catcher when throwing to the bases to nip runners

use a *Chicago Slide,* falling away from the base and hooking it with a toe

are in a *pickle* when caught between bases

make a *can of corn*—an easy flyball catch

are *Berlin Wallers* when as outfielders they climb the fence to make a tremendous catch

Other general terms:

Sweetheart   a headline-happy player

Yannigan   a rookie

Cuckoohead, whirlybird, moon man, airhead   an eccentric player

Bird dog   a scout

Corkscrew or *twirlythumb*   a left-handed player (now about 21% of all players)

Air Forcer   a much-traded athlete, with "more stops than the Air Force"

Pine-rider   a utility man spending much time on the bench

Fungo Man   a coach or player who specializes in lofting practice flyballs with a fungo stick

Stanza   one inning

Bad moss   a player going bald

Motorman   a speedy player

Bad wheels   a player with leg trouble

Orphans Wallop Beaneaters

If the above newspaper headline for a game report of the 1880s sounds weird, how about "Spiders Beat Plymouth Rocks" or "Bridegrooms Smash Rainmakers?" Over the past century, major loop teams have been named everything up to and including *White Elephants.*

Before the Los Angeles Dodgers were the Brooklyn Dodgers, they were called the *Bridegrooms* (a lot of married men on the roster?), *Superbas* and *Trolley Dodgers.* Boston's Red Sox evolved from *Speed Boys, Beaneaters* and *Plymouth Rocks.* Chicago's Cubs at various times went by the *Colts, Orphans, Cowboys* and *Rainmakers.* A pioneer Philadelphia club was sneered at by foes as the *White Elephants* (a box office flop). Defiantly sewing white elephant patches on team suits, the team rose to fame with a name change to *Athletics.* Now the old Philly A's are the pride of Oakland.

New York sportswriter **Jim Price** invented *Yankees,* after *Highlanders* (for a Scottish regiment) became unpopular. Manager **George Stallings** dressed his Detroit team in black-and-yellow socks in 1899 and it became forever after the *Tigers.* Cleveland's first teams went from *Spiders* (they crawled all over opponents) to *Naps* (for manager **Napoleon Lajoie**) before adopting the present *Indians.* Cincinnati was the first team to discard ankle-length pants for knicker-bockers, and their bright-red hose led to *Red Stockings, Redlegs* and, finally, *Reds.*

Fans and sportswriters in Philadelphia violently hated the tag of *Bluejays,* which was the winning suggestion in a public name-this-team contest. So the team owner gave in and plain old *Phillies* became permanent.

One club that found their name near the start was Pittsburgh. Coming into the National League in 1887, the team raided talent far and wide. Other teams screamed, "They're pirates." And *Pirates* it is to this day.

In 1902, the *New York Nationals* was good enough for a last-place team. By 1904, they were league champs and people began calling them *Giants.* As far as San Francisco is concerned, they still are.

MAJOR LEAGUE TEAMS

American League

Oakland A's 1901*
green, yellow
Oakland Alameda County Stadium

Seattle Mariners 1976
navy, yellow
Kingdome

California Angels 1961
red, blue, yellow
Anaheim Stadium

Texas Rangers 1972
orange, black
Arlington Stadium

Kansas City Royals 1973
blue, white
Royals Stadium

Minnesota Twins 1961
red, white, blue
Hubert H. Humphrey Metrodome

San Francisco Giants 1883
orange, black
Candlestick Park

Los Angeles Dodgers 1911
royal blue, white
Dodger Stadium

San Diego Padres 1969
brown, yellow
Jack Murphy Stadium

National League

*year given is the first year the team was called
by its present name

Chicago White Sox 1900
red, white, black
Comiskey Park

Milwaukee Brewers 1970
royal blue, yellow
Milwaukee County Stadium

Detroit Tigers 1895
orange, blue
Tiger Stadium

Cleveland Indians 1901
blue, red, white
Cleveland Stadium

Toronto Blue Jays 1976
light blue, royal, red
Exhibition Stadium

Baltimore Orioles 1885
orange, black
Memorial Stadium

New York Yankees 1913
blue, white
Yankee Stadium

Boston Red Sox 1901
red, black
Fenway Park

Houston Astros 1965
orange, yellow, blue
Astrodome

Chicago Cubs 1907
blue, white, red
Wrigley Field

St. Louis Cardinals 1899
red, navy
Busch Memorial Stadium

Cincinnati Reds 1869
red, white
Riverfront Stadium

Montreal Expos 1969
blue, red, white
Olympic Stadium

Atlanta Braves 1966
red, white, blue
Atlanta-Fulton County Stadium

Pittsburgh Pirates 1891
black, yellow
Three Rivers Stadium

Philadelphia Phillies 1883
red, white
Veterans Stadium

New York Mets 1960
royal blue, orange
Shea Stadium

SPRING TRAINING

Some veteran observers argue that spring training camps are a sham, a mammoth waste of money and are mostly conducted for publicity purposes.

"You take the show out of town, as with a Broadway play, then bring it back for Opening Day—and you've received millions of inches of free newspaper and magazine ink," complainers say.

Detroit Tigers manager **Sparky Anderson** retorts: "That's a lot of malarkey. Spring is when you condition guys who've grown fat and lazy over the winter. You run the hell out of them. Your top 2 dozen or so players will lose a combined 400 lbs under a hot sun, and a manager gets to take a close look at minor league prospects."

But it's true that spring training isn't cheap: some teams spend as much as $400,000 to feed, house and train the entire club, plus a good number of promising farm team players, through March and early April. Only about half this amount is recouped by the 1,500,000 exhibition game tickets sold nationwide during the practice season.

Spring training facilities tend to be luxurious. Perhaps the most splendid camp is the Los Angeles Dodgers' Vero Beach FL base, which is equipped with 3 playing fields, 8 batting cages, 6 pitcher's mounds, swimming pools, golf courses, a 5000-seat stadium and a cafeteria that serves steak, crepes and strawberries with cream.

Since manager **Cap Anson** of the Chicago Cubs set up the first formal spring training camp at Hot Springs AR in 1886, clubs have wandered far and wide in search of the perfect vernal hideaway. In 1906, **John McGraw** took his Giants to southern California—and ran into rainstorms. Seeking sea breezes, the Wrigley-owned Chicago Cubs trained at Wrigley-owned Catalina Island off the Los Angeles coast. Other teams in the 1920s liked New Orleans, while the Detroit Tigers cashed in on *Georgia Peach* Ty Cobb's fame by camping in Augusta GA. Some teams left the continent entirely: The 1911 Yankees trained on Bermuda's coral strand.

Branch Rickey discovered Florida in 1914, with its ideal weather and large numbers of senior citizens ready to buy tickets to St. Louis Browns' exhibition games. Today, 18 of the 26 major league teams train in the *Grapefruit League.* Arizona became a popular training ground after World War II, and now the *Cactus League* hosts the rest of the teams.

Grapefruit League (Florida):

1	Philadelphia Phillies	Clearwater
2	Cincinnati Reds	Tampa
3	Pittsburgh Pirates	Bradenton
4	Chicago White Sox	Sarasota
5	Minnesota Twins	Orlando
6	Boston Red Sox	Winter Haven
7	St. Louis Cards	St. Petersburg
8	Houston Astros	Cocoa Beach
9	Baltimore Orioles	Miami
10	Montreal Expos	West Palm Beach
11	Toronto Blue Jays	Dunedin
12	Detroit Tigers	Lakeland
13	Los Angeles Dodgers	Vero Beach
14	Texas Rangers	Pompano Beach
15	New York Mets	St. Petersburg
16	New York Yankees	Ft. Lauderdale
17	Atlanta Braves	West Palm Beach
18	Kansas City Royals	Ft. Myers

Cactus League (Arizona):

19	California Angels	Palm Springs CA
20	Seattle Mariners	Tempe
21	Milwaukee Brewers	Sun City
22	San Francisco Giants	Scottsdale
23	Cleveland Indians	Tuscon
24	Chicago Cubs	Mesa
25	Oakland A's	Phoenix
26	San Diego Padres	Yuma

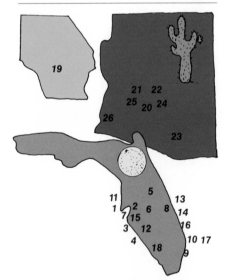

UMPIRES

"Umpires got to be stupid to begin with or they wouldn't take the job," an American League manager once said on a long, losing afternoon. "Even when they're right, they're wrong. Would you want your daughter to marry one?"

Most dugout denizens would agree with that. But if these bad guys in blue, these loneliest men in sports, these (to the fan) certified thieves are so dumb, how do we explain this:

Average pay of umps
1950s: $6500 per season.
1972: $11,500 minimum plus an incease from $3000 to $8000 per man for working the World Series.

1975: $14,500 starting income for rookie officials; up to $36,000 for a 20-year man, plus a pension plan and $9500 for the Series.
1977: beginning pay of $16,000, ranging up to $40,000 for a veteran; $49 per diem traveling expenses.
1983: starting salary of $26,000, going up to $70,000 for senior umpires; per diem

expenses of $77; $10,000 per man for working a championship playoff game and $15,000 per man for the World Series.

Seventy thousand bucks for going to baseball games! Who says umps aren't smart?

That quantum leap in less than a decade was secured by the 1968 formation of the **Major League Umpires Association,** which staged strikes in 1970 and 1979 and won concessions and respect from the game's leaders. From a position of poor, downtrodden cops on the beat only 25 seasons ago, umps have risen in stature as well as salary, and now call a lot of the shots in their profession:

The MLUA forced sale of ballpark drinks in paper cups, eliminating the need for officials to duck potentially lethal bottles.

An ump no longer has to drag 75-80 lbs of equipment around from city to city; the NL and AL pay for the shipment of pads, masks, shinguards and uniforms by express air.

In 1974, the MLUA won the right for its members to wear eyeglasses (never mind the barrage of jokes)—just as some players do.

Umpires now draw a pension at the rate of $1000 for every year of service, and have an in-season, 2-week paid vacation.

Once, a hotheaded Cub named **Dolf Luque** attacked umpire *Babe* Pinelli with an icepick. Such antics can't happen today—security men surround the arbitrators after the game.

Baseball has at last admitted in a practical way that it can't function without a prosperous corps of strong law enforcers on the beat, that without them there'd be total chaos, and that nobody works much harder than the umps. They oversee 162 games in a 180-day season, or about 1400 innings a year. In one typical 9-inning game, the 4 officials:

call 280-300 balls and strikes
call 65-70 runners safe or out on bases
call 15-20 men safe or out at first base
are twice clobbered by a foul ball or
 otherwise hit and hurt

2 op puck off tops?

Although TV's instant replay occasionally shows an umpire to have erred on a decision, it's calculated that an infielder would have to play about 30 flawless games to face as many opportunities to be right or wrong as a plate ump has in just one. "A batter would have to hit safely between 18-20 times straight to be as accurate as we are," points out veteran arbitrator **Bill Haller** of the American League.

Ballplayers who define an ump's mistake as any call that goes against them continue a 1980s trend toward getting physical with the blueboys. They bump, spit upon and sometimes shove them. In retaliation, the thumbs of ejection rise more often these days. Fans who study their TV screens detect a new grimness among the MLUA members. "Umps are meaner than I've ever seen them," is the running comment in dugouts. Adds Boston Red Sox manager **Ralph Houk,** who has been bounced from more than a few contests for complaining too hotly, "Umps are a lot taller and heftier than in the past—some are giants."

There is truth in Houk's observation. Not long ago, a lot of skinny little guys in caps populated the majors' home plates and

basepaths, but now, while there's no official NL or AL height requirement, big bruisers tougher than penitentiary guards are preferred. Size helps equalize the fact that 4 umps are outnumbered by 18 players, 2 managers and assorted coaches. Some current examples:

John McSherry (NL)	6'3"	250 lbs
Jim McKean (AL)	6'2"	225 lbs
Harry Wendelstedt (NL)	6'2"	230 lbs
Lee Weyer (AL)	6'6"	260 lbs
Joe West (NL)	6'1"	220 lbs
Bill Haller (AL)	6'4"	210 lbs
Vic Voltaggio (AL)	6'4"	210 lbs
Satch Davidson (NL)	6'2"	210 lbs
Greg Kosc (AL)	6'2"	240 lbs

Of the 56 umpires on NL and AL rosters as of 1983, 43 stand 6' or more. In 1980 the NL's **Eric Gregg,** one of the few black officials to reach the big leagues, weighed 357 lbs! He was called *Fat Albert* after a character created by comedian **Bill Cosby.** The New York Mets padded themselves with towels in his honor. The Montreal Expos served him a 2'-long sandwich at home plate.

Enough was enough. Gregg went on a strict diet and lost 106 lbs, and now balances out at a svelte 280. But he's still fearsome, despite his reduced size: "Not too many people challenge me," he says.

But when you're dealing with increasingly beefy ballplayers, it helps to be big. **George Magerkurth,** a legendary 270-pounder, once put a player in the hospital with one punch. **Ron Luciano,** 6'4" and 250 lbs, threatened to slug manager **Billy Martin** during a 1974 altercation, then cocked his fist. "Don't hit me!" cried Martin—despite his impressive reputation as a fistfighter. Luciano easily won that round.

The former and off-season careers of the men who break up field fights and duck foul tips show just how tough they are:
Jim McKean (AL) is an ex-pro football player.
Dick Garcia (AL) is an ex-Marine.
Nick Colosi (NL) is a special police officer.
George Maloney (AL) earned 5 battle stars.
Ed Vargo (NL) is a probation officer.
Ken Kaiser (AL) is an ex-heavyweight wrestler.

While managers are fired at a furious rate, officials stay on and on. The NL now has a pair of 20-year men, and the AL has 4. Many more have stayed for 15 years or more. The all-time record is 37 years, held by the NL's **Bill Klem,** whose career began in 1905 and ended in 1941. **Tom Connolly** of the AL umpired for 34 years. Both are in the Hall of Fame.

Deaf-mute **Dummy Taylor,** *who pitched for New York between 1900-1908, was once thrown out of a game for cursing at an umpire—in sign language.*

Umpires categorize the complainers 3 ways:
1 **The chronic kicker** *continually moans and groans over strike calls. "This type beefs without turning his head to us—otherwise, we might go tell him to soak his head in the showers," say the umps.*
2 **The alibi kicker** *puts on a show to persuade fans he's right. His repertoire includes Charlie Chaplin's doubletakes, Jack Benny's slackjawed stare and Bugs Bunny's hysterical outbreaks.*
3 **The surveyor** *uses his hands and bat to explain where the strike zone, home plate and batter's box are located. "A .250 hitter, usually, who couldn't find his way home after dark," the officials snort.*

| play ball | do not pitch | player is out | | runner is safe | | delayed ball dead |
| | time out | | infield fly | | ball dead | |

Once upon a time, the Brooklyn Dodgers' "Sym-Phony Band" raised umpires' hackles. This horn-blasting, skillet-clanging gang always played *Three Blind Mice* when the umpires appeared at game time. Although such independent orchestral ensembles are discouraged today, park organists have been known to render *Dancing in the Dark, I Got Plenty O' Nuthin'* or *You're Driving Me Crazy.* More recently, umpires' pet peeves include:

San Diego Padres' chicken mascot His act includes choking an umpire dummy before the cheering throng.

TV replays At one time, a blown call was noticed only by the fans in the park, but now millions of TV viewers can watch errors repeated 2 or 3 times on instant replay—and the boos rise nationwide.

Spitball throwers For decades, umps have tried to catch pitchers in the act of gooping up the ball—and almost never succeeded. Umpire **Augie Donatelli** became so frustrated once that he yanked off Dodger **Don Drysdale's** cap, grabbed a handful of hair and claimed he found grease. Drysdale had to shampoo between innings.

Managers such as now-retired **Earl Weaver,** who was tossed out of more than 80 games and suspended 4 times. Retired ump **Ron Luciano** says, "Managers holler for 3 reasons—they think we erred, they're trying to keep a player from being run out and, most frequent, they're temporarily insane."

Duties
Umpires in both leagues travel in units of 4. Though each team has a senior *crew chief,* the members take turns at each position by rotating clockwise around the diamond each day. Their job actually begins about 2 hours before game time:

Step 1 Factory-fresh baseballs are too slick, so the crews rub them with a special mud that removes the gloss without dirtying the leather.

Step 2 One ump takes a seat in the stands, acting as a spy to make sure there's no *fraternizing* (players talking to each other). Umps hate this duty, but league rules state there can be no sign of amity between teams.

Step 3 The crew goes over the ground rules with managers, who know every nook and cranny of the park but usually find something to argue about anyway. Espionage (stealing signs with binoculars hidden in the outfield) often comes up.

Step 4 The 3rd base umpire carries a bag of 4 dozen balls to the plate for distribution to the plate ump (the *saddlebags* on his hips can hold 6 at a time) and to the ballboys. Balls are thrown out of the game for any little discoloration or chip (hang the expense) and sometimes 48 aren't enough in an extra-inning contest.

When an umpire cleans off home plate, he never does it with his fanny facing the crowd. It's not the gentlemanly thing to do. Long tradition holds that he walks clear around the catcher and batter to face the audience while doing his housecleaning: the big leagues, if anything, are classy.

Step 5 Crewmen scatter to their positions. The 1st base ump works behind and close to the base, so he can be on top of the 20 or more *out* and *safe* calls that are made per game. The 2nd base ump positions himself behind the basepath between 2nd and 3rd bases for fast access to both the outfield on a flyball and a tag at 2nd. The 3rd base man straddles the chalkline 8-10' behind the bag to gain a head start on balls hit to left field while remaining flexible on base-tags. The plate umpire's position behind the catcher varies between the AL and NL.

Equipment
Face mask Heavier than the catcher's flip-off mask, it has double bars to shield against fouls but leaves ample room through which to peer. Umps buy their own masks for about $45.

Throat-protector or **goatee** A heavy leather latch suspended from the mask's bottom to guard the throat. It comes with the mask.

Chest protector At one time AL men wore the bulky, inflated, outside-the-jacket *balloon pad* and the NL men used an *inside* protector. Now more than 90% of all umpires in both leagues favor the inside model, since the balloon type gets in the way when they crouch to call low pitches. It costs $80 when custom-fitted; they buy their own.

Shoes These come low-cut and laced for speedy movement, but with a thick piece of leather sewn over the instep and a steel toe. Officials pay $75-$100 for shoes.

Shinguards Not as big as the catcher's, since they are worn under the pants. They run around $30 per set and are paid for by the umps.

whiskbroom is that, when a batter is beefing and using foul language, the ump can call time, and while cleaning the plate, quietly advise, "Don't say one more word or you're out of here."

Pen and scorepad Used by the ump at the plate for keeping track of lineup changes and other data.

Strategy
Refined over many years, there's much more to the umpire's task than meets the casual eye. Bulwarking this refinement are the rules, which give umps complete autonomy. *Rule 9.01(a)* gives them authority for conduct of games, and holds that any decision involving *judgment* (strike or pitch, fair or foul ball, safe or out) may not be appealed and is final. *Rule 9.01(d)*, the *take-a-hike* edict, empowers umpires to eject anyone at all from the premises.

That's practically total power. Teams can protest, but the protests are almost always denied. Self-respect is the umpire's #1 stock-in-trade, especially where foul language is concerned. "If they tell me I'm blinder than a potato with 40 eyes, or use unoriginal obscenities, I just smile and the game goes on." says one official. "But if they ever question my geneaology, I run them out."

Here's the *modus operandi* of the guys we love to hate:

Balls and Strikes The home plate umpire sets up an imaginary 2-dimensional rectangular *window* for pitches—the *strike zone.* This area is defined by the space over the plate between the batter's armpits and the top of his knees when he adopts his natural batting stance. The zone varies: A pair of 6-footers may have the same strike zone, but for an erect **Mike Schmidt** it may be larger than for a crouching **Pete Rose.** For a croucher, the umpire adjusts his window—but the crouch must be a habitual one.

Uniforms The NL and AL supply 2 blue blazers and 2 pairs of grey slacks. They also provide 2 powder blue shirts, 3 undershirts, 2 cotton-acrylic turtleneck sweaters and a pair of caps. The ump's number appears on both the shortsleeve summer shirts and the blazers. At $450 per man, this is about a $25,000 annual tab for the AL and NL. Until the 1960s, officials wore drab, baggy serge suits; fortunately, the fashion changed and brought with it creased slacks, tailored coats, caps resembling those of the players—and no more beanies.

Longjohns Cold-weather underwear like lumberjacks wear. Goliath-sized umpires need to have them specially tailored.

Ball-and-strike indicator This little gadget has saved many an arbitrator from mixing up the count on the batter. Indicators have 3 manually operated wheels. For a strike, the wheel is pushed away from the ump; for a ball it's pushed toward him. The third wheel indicates the number of outs.

Whiskbroom For plate-cleaning. A top-quality whisk can last for years. One ump, **Bill Stewart,** clung to his so long that it was worn to a near-stub. Another value of the

Just as there are 3 types of grousing players, there are 3 types of umpires. A longtime member of the fraternity, **Ralph** *Babe* **Pinelli,** *identified them as:*
"Hard noses who are belligerent and come to work with a chip on their shoulders. They fail to let players blow their tops a little and promote more trouble."
"Nice Guys who are sincere, but lack real ability for the job and have to fake their way at times. Their lives become hell and after a while they quit."
"Real pros, slow-to-anger fast thinkers who have the rule book down pat, react in a flash and will listen to arguments—up to a well-specified point. You can yell, but don't ever question their heritage."
Babe Pinelli was the latter type. In 22 years he ejected only 42 demonstrators—an amazingly low number.

When the designated hitter rule came into effect in the American League in 1973, the first DH to step to bat was **Ron Blomberg,** *lefthanded hitting Yankee outfielder with a .320 average. On that same day, 6 April 1973,* **Tony Oliva** *of the Minnesota Twins delivered the first home run by a DH.*

No member of the Major League Umpires Association has ever been found guilty of fixing a game or other dishonorable conduct. Only one case of a cheating umpire has ever been recorded: Back in 1882, one **Dick Higham** *was found to be tipping gamblers on how to bet on games he was working, and was immediately banned from the game.*

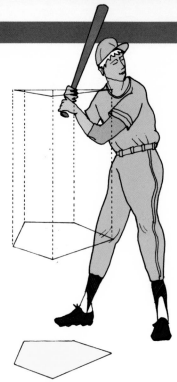

For many years, NL umpires have recognized a lower strike zone than their AL counterparts. In the NL, a borderline pitch around the knees is much more likely to be called a strike. A pitch above the letters is more likely to be an AL strike. Low-ball hitters thus fare better on the National circuit than American. How much difference is there? "As much as 2 inches," estimates San Francisco Giants manager **Frank Robinson,** who starred in both leagues.

Sinking liner While an outfielder sprints to make a shoestring catch, the base ump runs off at a tangent to the play, not toward it. This gives him a better line on the path of the descending ball and a better angle to determine whether it was caught in the air or trapped on the ground.

The half swing This is the most difficult of all plate judgments. Did the batter swing or check his bat in time? This action isn't a matter of *breaking the wrists* on the swing, as most fans believe. The decision rests on whether or not he made a "bona fide attempt to hit the ball." One set of eyes often can't decide this, so since 1975 the umpires at 1st and 3rd bases may be appealed to by either team to uphold or reverse the plateman's call. Field umps have a better angle on a half-swing in most cases than the plateman.

First base calls It often seems that runner and ball arrive at the sack just about simultaneously. Positioned to see *into* the play, the 1st base umpire watches the runner's lead foot as it strikes the bag while listening for the slap of the ball into the 1st baseman's mitt. *Bang-bang* plays go to the runner if it's a tie.

Foul pop-up The riskiest play for the plateman. His technique is to pivot away from the pop, giving the catcher unimpeded room. When the catcher flings his mask away, the ump must be prepared to duck that flying object, too.

Double play The high-speed pivot of an infielder at 2nd base is often controversial, since an optical illusion can exist for fans. They think the fielder traveled over the bag before taking the throw from another fielder. His continuing motion fools viewers who can't hear the smack of the ball hitting the glove at the instant the fielder's foot touches the bag. Some 2nd basemen and shortstops kick back to the bag while making the pivot-throw to 1st. To the crowd, this is an illegal *phantom double play,* but the umpire is at an angle to look *into* the scene and *split* the action. The *1 yard rule* is used on runners who slide in outside the baseline to knock down or otherwise impede the fielder's throw to home plate: If they stray more than 3' off a direct line to the bag, they're out.

Nolan Ryan delivered the fastest ball ever in 1974 — a blistering 108 mph.

The plate ump is positioned differently in the AL and NL. The National officials work from a stance between the catcher and the batter called *the slot,* from which they see pitches at a tangent. American Leaguers see pitches straight on from their stance directly in back of the catcher, staring over his head and shoulders.

The Baseball Hall of Fame includes 3 umpires. They are **Billy Evans, Cal Hubbard** and:

Close plays at the plate Again the umpire, depending upon where the catcher sets up to take a throw; gets an angle on the play. He must dance in close—because of kicked-up dust and tangled limbs—to insure that the runner touches the plate before the ball is slapped on some part of his body. Meanwhile, he must nimbly avoid getting rammed into by the sliding runner. One official, **Lou DiMuro,** was hit by a 200-lb slider who veered off at the last instant. DiMuro was badly hurt and out for the remainder of the season.

Tag play: Even if the ball clearly beats the runner to the sack, the ump makes sure the base is protected (contacted) while the tag is applied. The *way* the tag is made decides the issue. A low squat is used to zero in on reaching arms and flying feet.

Attempted steals The base ump watches the shortstop and 2nd baseman let each other know who's going to cover the middle base on a steal try by flashing an open glove. The base umpire then concentrates on the infielder taking the catcher's throw.

Jocko Conlan, elected to the Hall of Fame in 1974, played with the White Sox until one day in 1935 when the umpire passed out from the heat. He stepped in to finish the game, and the rest, as they say, is history.

mouth, not glove

Greats
Asked to single out the best umpires, ballplayers grow shy: ump-hatred makes it hard for them to pick the best of the breed. But in one 1983 poll by the *New York Times,* a few favorites did emerge. Every player on the major league roster was asked for an opinion, and 72% turned in their responses:

Tom Connolly was an Englishman who was known as a walking rule book during his 34 years as an official.

AL Husky **Steve Palermo**—called *strict* and *accurate*—was ranked #1. Palermo, an umpire for over a decade, hails from Worcester MA. **Rich Garcia,** of Key West FL, and **Dave Phillips,** who has worked many championship and World Series games over 16 seasons, were the second favorites.

NL Laurence Henry *Dutch* **Rennert, Jr.** was named the players' first choice. Rennert has been around since 1973, and the 5'8" Oshkosh WI native was described as *plenty tough, but fair.* Behind Rennert ranked **Doug Harvey** and **Ed Vargo,** both of whom have been around over a quarter of a century.

Dirty Business: The Mud
In 1938, **Russell A.** *Lena* **Blackburne,** a Philadelphia A's coach, noticed umpires rubbing the factory gloss off balls with field dirt and water. The junk left scratches on the cover, and Lena looked for something better. In a secret spot, believed to have been on the Delaware River (but now suspected to be somewhere in south New Jersey), Blackburne found a unique mud containing an ultra-fine abrasive that left covers unmarred. Forming the Lena Blackburne Rubbing Mud Co., he grew prosperous selling his gunk to the big leagues at $15 and then $20 per coffee can. To this day, Lena's mud remains the only authorized goo for taking the slick off new balls—a job that keeps umpires busy before games.

Bill Klem was an umpire's umpire—probably the greatest in baseball history. The arm signals used by today's officials were invented by Klem, who stood behind home plate at 18 World Series.

In the course of a 9-inning game, a major league manager may need to make 40 to 50 quick, win-or-lose decisions.

This characteristic of the job means that managers must be powerful thinkers who can instantly commit themselves to a decision—and makes them the most often-fired men in pro sports.

In the 1980s, an average of over 40% of AL and NL bench chiefs are discharged every season, although canned managers usually find work with another owner, since baseball believes in recycling its field generals. For example, **Whitey Herzog,** now commanding the St. Louis Cards, previously managed at Washington DC, Kansas City, Baltimore and Detroit. **Dick Williams** has bounced from Boston to Oakland to Anaheim to Montreal to San Diego.

To avoid the sack and win at least 80 of the 162 games in a season, managers must weigh an astonishing number of factors with computerlike versatility. Among the most crucial are:

Lineup In picking the day's starting players, the manager puts his best *on-base* men at the #1 lead-off and #2 lineup positions. They're skilled at bunting, placing hits, drawing walks and stealing bags. At the 3, 4 and 5 slots are the big cannons, the run-producers. But if a slugger is in a slump, should he be dropped to #6 for the moment, with a utility man or hot rookie replacing him higher up? A hard decision, indeed.

Starting pitcher The orthodox thinking is that a left-hander is wanted against a strongly left-handed hitting team, and vice versa. But the manager must assess the skills of each member of his pitching staff, taking into account the pitcher's condition, the duration since his last game, and the particular challenges presented by different opponents.

Relief pitching Managers must hoard their bullpen of pitching reserves, since starters frequently last only 3-6 innings. Then they must choose a *long reliever* to take over the bulk of the remaining game, often to be followed by *short relievers,* who finish the final innings. Personnel juggling is an art.

Bench strength Knowing his options is a key part of the manager's game. Who does he insert as a pinch-hitter, or on defense, or as a pinch runner? When should he make substitutions?

Opponent Bench bosses must know to the decimal point the offensive-defensive skills of the other club, anticipate the other manager's moves, and plan countermoves innings ahead.

Signals The 1st and 3rd base coaches are the manager's signal relay men on the field. They go through a comedic collection of contortions as they slap hands, touch their uniform or skin, tug trousers, rub ears and otherwise pass on to team members the signs for the next tactical move. Most coaching semaphore is fake, with the real sign hidden in all the gesticulating. Managers usually sit in a far corner of the bench, as far out of enemy view as possible to frustrate sign-stealing by spies across the way. As a further foil against espionage, managers may use a bench-riding player, a trainer, or even a 14-year-old batboy to send the signals for them.

Unexpected plays Daring managers will go *against the book* (favorable percentages) at odd times, having a batter swing away on an automatic *take* count of 3-0 (3 balls, no strikes), or having a catcher drop a bunt.

These managers rank among the all-time greatest, based on overall record, player-handling skills, championship game performance and durability.

George Lee *Sparky* Anderson Some assert that **Earl Weaver** (now retired) or **Billy Martin** ranks #1 among modern strategists, but we prefer Sparky Anderson. The Cincinnati Reds were also-rans until Anderson came along and drove them to NL championships in 1970, 72, 73, 75 and 76, and 2 winning Series. Now with Detroit, Anderson put the Tigers in the running for the pennant in 1983. With 1200 career victories, he's the winningest active manager.

Charles Dillon *Casey* Stengel The *Old Professor's* image was that of the clown, but during his 25 years as a manager he took the Yankees to 10 pennants and 7 World Series, including 5 consecutive Series wins between 1949-53. Stengel's wizardry was based on his knowledge of when to let a player go and who to replace him with. He managed until he was 65, the second-longest career in the big leagues.

John J. McGraw A fiery taskmaster, McGraw still holds the record for most World Series wins—10. Between 1902-1932, he made the New York Giants a feared force. Stressing the bunt and the steal, *Black John* won 3 straight NL pennants and lasted 33 years at the top of his field.

The first night game ever was played on 24 May 1935 at Crosley Field in Cincinnati. The Reds beat the Philadelphia Phillies 2-1.

Walter Emmons Alston Big and tough enough to punch out any bad-boy player, Alston is one of only 6 managers whose teams won more than 2000 games. In 23 seasons, he led the Brooklyn and Los Angeles Dodgers to 7 NL flags and 4 World Series triumphs.

Cornelius *Connie Mack* **McGillicuddy** At 6'4", the *Tall Tactician* was the most elegant and durable of managers—he was still moving fielders around with a twitch of his scorecard in 1950 at the age of 88. He won his first pennant with the Philadelphia A's (which he owned) in 1902. Noted for wearing civilian clothes in the dugout, Mack accumulated a record 3776 lifetime victories during his unequaled 53-year career.

Leo Ernest Durocher Hate him or love him, no one can deny that *Leo the Lip* motivated teams as well as any manager ever did. In 24 seasons, he accumulated over 2000 career wins. A hell-raiser, Durocher kicked umps, was suspended, got fired, and was attacked by the press, but his New York Giants topped the NL 3 times. **Willie Mays** said, "Leo made me a star."

Other managers, past and present, who left their mark on the game (followed by number of years of service): **Miller Huggins** (16), **Bucky Harris** (29), **Bill McKechnie** (25), **Jimmy Dykes** (31), **Cap Anson** (20), **Charlie Grimm** (20), **Joe Cronin** (17), **Billy Southworth** (13), **Chuck Dressen** (13), **Red Schoendienst** (12), **Ralph Houk** (18), **Dick Williams** (15), and **Billy Martin** (15).

It's widely known that Babe Ruth was No.3 and Lou Gehrig was No.4—but who was the first big-leaguer to wear a number on his back? He was **Earl Averill** *of the Cleveland Indians, who wore No.5 on 6 April 1929. The Indians had experimented with numbers on uniform sleeves way back in 1916. Now they introduced full back numbering—and Averill celebrated the occasion his first time at bat with a home run!*

The commissioners of Organized Baseball have been a strangely mixed assortment of personalities.

The job was envisioned as one of ultimate power, but more often the baseball commissioner has been a pawn in the political games of club owners. Successful commissioners walk a fine line, since they must aggressively police the very people who give them power, and the job takes an exacting toll: one former commissioner died in office, another was forced to resign, a third was fired outright and the latest quit in barely disguised disgust.

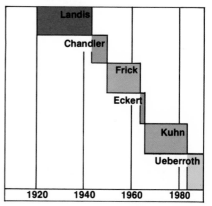

The current commissioner is **Peter V. Ueberroth,** a California travel entrepreneur who gained the attention of the sporting world as the head of the Los Angeles Olympic Organizing Committee. He earned a reputation as a financial wizard by developing a new way to finance the Games (which had historically exhausted the funds of host cities) through large-scale corporate support, and encouraged the city to use already-existing facilities for Olympic events rather than invest public funds in new complexes. Ueberroth will continue predecessor **Bowie Kuhn's** efforts at keeping major league baseball popular—and, consequently, solvent. To this end, he demanded unprecedented concessions from the owners before he agreed to take the job—concessions that greatly expand the clout carried by the commissioner. Ueberroth has the authority to fine a club up to $250,000 (the previous limit was $5000); both league presidents now report directly to him; and he can be re-elected by a vote of 14 of the 26 owners (formerly, a commissioner was elected by a ⅔ majority in each league).

Ueberroth is the sixth man to hold the title of Commissioner of Baseball. His predecessors were:

Contrary to popular belief, **Jackie Robinson** *was not the first black man ever to play pro baseball. That distinction actually belongs to* **Moses Fleetwood Walker,** *who was a catcher for Toledo (then a major league team) between 1883-1889. Walker's brother,* **Welday Wilberforce Walker,** *was among more than a dozen black players who followed him to the the big time before pressure from several popular white players (most notably* **Cap Anson**) *led the raising of the color barrier in 1887—a barrier that stood for 60 years.*

Kenesaw Mountain Landis (1920-1944) Baseball was in chaos, reeling from repeated scandals and bitter feuds, when the National Commission was abolished and the job of Commissioner was created. Landis, a Chicago judge of fierce reputation, was given a $65,000 salary and absolute power to do anything needed to save the integrity of baseball. He permanently banned any player suspected of association with gamblers and unhesitatingly fined clubs who violated his rules. Landis ruled with an iron hand until he died of a heart attack after 24 years of service.

Albert B. *Happy* Chandler (1945-1951) A US senator from Kentucky, Chandler improved the status of umpires and ended the blacklist against players who jumped to the rich Mexican League. But Chandler lacked Landis' dignified stature, and was frequently seen betting money at racetracks. He made a few legal errors and many enemies in high places, and was asked to resign after serving only 6 years.

Ford C. Frick (1951-1965) Former New York sportswriter, radio broadcaster and NL president, Frick was considered by many—most especially the players—to be a creature of the owners. The highlight of his long but uneventful tenure was the Supreme Court's decision to uphold baseball's 1922 anti-trust exemption.

General William D. Eckert (1965-1968) Obviously looking for another controllable commissioner, the owners elected an obscure Air Force general to succeed Frick. Eckert served largely in a ceremonial capacity and avoided all controversy, but was fired anyway in 1968.

Bowie Kent Kuhn (1969-1984) The most interesting character to hold the post since Landis died, the 6′5″ Kuhn was an NL attorney when elected to replace Eckert. Under Kuhn, the majors expanded to 26 teams and were split into divisions. He fostered highly lucrative media contracts for the championship and World Series games, but was accused of doing little to avert the 1981 players' strike. Kuhn's attempts to exercise his power against the owners (he fined Yankees owner **George Steinbrenner** $50,000 for misconduct in 1983, following an earlier suspension) led him to resign in apparent disgust later that year.

RULES

Hardcore baseball fans revel in details of the sport's long and glorious history, the precision of the thousands of statistics and the subtleties of the rule book; sometimes it seems that there's so much to know that a novice could never understand or enjoy the game.

But the basic idea of baseball is really quite easy to grasp—one of the reasons it's become a worldwide favorite.

Baseball is played on a shell-shaped field with a 90′ square, or *diamond*, marked at the apex. A *base* is set at each corner of the diamond; going counterclockwise, they are *1st base, 2nd base, 3rd base* and *home plate*. The bases are marked by small, heavy canvas pillows attached to the ground. The area within the square is called the *infield;* territory beyond the bases but between the 2 *foul lines* is the *outfield.*

Two teams of 9 players each take turns as the *batting* (offensive) team and the *fielding* (defensive) team.

Offense
The goal of the batting team is to score *runs*. A run is accomplished when a player makes one complete circuit of the three bases and returns to home plate *safely*. The offensive team sends players to bat in a consecutive, pre-arranged order. The *batter* stands at home plate and attempts to hit the baseball, thrown toward him by the other team's *pitcher*. Batters are only required to hit pitches that fall in the *strike zone*, an imaginary window over home plate that extends from the batter's knees to his shoulders. A pitcher must be very skilled to place the ball within the strike zone yet still elude the bat. Pitches that fall outside the

strike zone are called *balls;* 4 balls allow the batter to advance or *walk* to 1st base. *Strikes* occur in any of 3 circumstances: **a)** the batter refuses to swing at a ball pitched through the strike zone, **b)** the batter swings at any thrown ball but misses or **c)** the batter *fouls off the pitch*—hits it into foul territory—when he has no more than one strike against him already. A batter is allowed 3 strikes; on his third strike he is *out* and his turn at bat ends.

A batter is *safe* at a base if, after hitting the ball along the ground or into the air, he reaches the base before the defenders can *field* (catch) the ball and throw it to that base. If the fielders get the ball to the player guarding the base before the runner gets there, the runner is out.

A *single* is a hit enabling a batter to safely reach 1st base. A *double* puts him on 2nd base, and a triple allows him to reach 3rd. A *home run* is scored when the batter hits the ball far enough—often over the field's fence—that he can run around the entire circle of bases before the ball can be successfully fielded. If the batter hits a home run when the *bases are loaded* (i.e., there are runners on 1st, 2nd and 3rd bases), then he and the other 3 runners all advance to home plate: 4 runs are scored, a *grand slam!*

Through hits by the offense's batters and *errors* in fielding by the defensive players, a team continues to advance its runners around the 4 bases in succession until it accumulates 3 outs. At this time, the teams switch places: the fielders get their turn at bat (and perhaps a chance to score) while the batters move onto the field and become defenders.

When each team has had a chance to both field and bat, the *inning* is over. A game consists of 9 innings; if the score is tied after that, extra innings are played until one team wins.

Defense

The defensive team tries to prevent the batting team from scoring runs. To achieve this, they assume these positions:

Pitcher The key man of the game. All eyes are on him as he subtly varies his pitches to make the batter miss.

Catcher He crouches behind the batter at home plate and catches pitches passed, missed or fouled by the batter. He also defends home plate against incoming runners and throws the ball to the other bases to help put out advancing runners.

1st, 2nd and **3rd basemen.** When the batter gets a fair hit and begins running to 1st base, the opposing team tries to catch the ball and get it to the 1st baseman before the batter/runner gets on base. If the runner reaches the base before the 1st baseman catches the ball and touches the bag, he is *safe* and allowed to remain. But if the runner arrives after the ball, he is out. This race between ball and runner is repeated at 2nd and 3rd base. Basemen must also be on guard against runners who try to *steal* bases—that is, advance to the next base by stealth, not by the next batter's hit or walk.

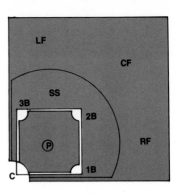

Shortstop A quick, versatile player stationed behind and between 2nd and 3rd bases. He acts as a connection between the outfielders and infielders, firing the ball quickly to any baseman who may be able to put out an oncoming runner. He also backs up the 2nd baseman in covering the base.

Outfielders (right, left and **center field)** These 3 players stand out beyond the bases to catch long hits. They can get an opponent out by catching a *fly ball* (a ball that is hit high into the air) before it touches the ground, or by quickly relaying a ball to the baseman before the runner gets there safely. The center fielder, with the most territory to cover, needs to be especially swift and have a strong throwing arm.

Designated hitter. The American League allows this 10th man on a team. The *DH* does not play defensively, but bats in place of the pitcher, who concentrates his efforts on pitching and is usually a weak hitter.

SCORING

Baseball, with its slow tempo, is ideally suited to the home scorekeeper.

Although many different scoring methods are used, here's one way to enjoy the game while keeping an inning-by-inning account:

1 You will need 2 scorecards (one for each team), a pencil, a comfortable chair, chips, sandwiches, a 6-pack of your favorite beverage, and this book. Several kinds of scorecards are available through book or sporting goods stores.

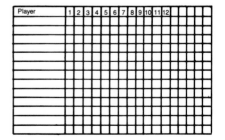

2 The blocks are arranged in a grid. Enter the positions, names and numbers of each team's players in their batting order in the columns provided. Batting order is announced at the beginning of the game.

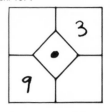
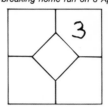

Scorecard showing **Hank Aaron's** *record-breaking home run on 8 April 1974*

3 Each inning block, or box, is divided into 5 parts representing a map of the diamond. The lower right corner represents 1st base, the upper right 2nd base, the upper left 3rd base and the lower left home plate. A single block shows one player's movement during a given inning. Each player is represented on the chart by a number, which is used to show how he reached base or was retired:

1 *pitcher*		**6** *shortstop*
2 *catcher*		**7** *left field*
3 *1st base*		**8** *center field*
4 *2nd base*		**9** *right field*
5 *3rd base*		**DH** *designated hitter*

4 These symbols are used to record events:

Single	1b
Double	2b
Triple	3b
Home run	HR
Walk	BB (base on balls)
Hit by pitch	HP
Intentional walk	IBB
Error	E
Bunt	B
Fielder's choice	FC
Stolen base	SB
Wild pitch	WP
Balk	BK
Sacrifice hit or fly	SH, SF
Strikeout swinging	K
Strikeout called	И
Put out while stealing	OS
Forceout	FO
Double play	DP
Triple play	TP
Foul fly	FF
Pop-up fly	P
Fly out	F

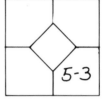
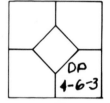

5 To show how a runner advances around the bases, enter the hitter's number in the box denoting the base the runner ended up on. For example, if a player starting on 1st base gets safely to 2nd on a hit by his team's first baseman, a 3 (the 1st baseman's position number) is entered in the upper right (2nd base) section of the runner's chart. If he's then batted home by the right fielder (9), a 9 is placed in the lower left part of the block, and the dot (representing a run) is put in the center.

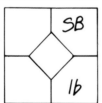

Infield outs are easy to show. If a 3rd baseman fields a ball and throws it to 1st base to make the out, you record it as 5-3. If the batter hits into a double play, 2nd base to shortstop to 1st base, it's DP 4-6-3.

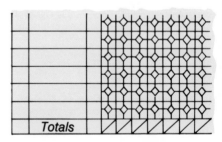

6 At the bottom of the page is the *Totals* line. Enter the number of runs per inning in the upper section of the box; the number of hits in the lower section.

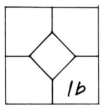
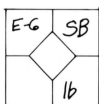
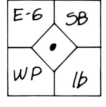

In this example, the batter singled to get on 1st base (represented by the *1b* in the lower right corner); stole 2nd base (shown as *SB* in the upper right corner); advanced to 3rd base on an error by the shortstop (*E-6* in the upper left corner) and scored on a wild pitch (*WP* in the box denoting home plate). The dot in the center diamond shows at a glance that a run was scored.

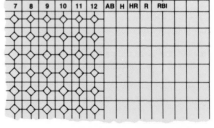

7 Many scorecards provide extra columns at the far right to record at-bats (AB), runs (R), hits (H), home runs (HR) and runs batted in (RBI) so you can record an individual player's performance in each of these areas at the end of the game. Use these figures to make comparisons between players and teams from game to game and year to year.

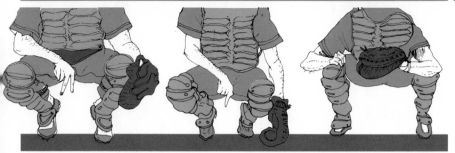

Catcher's Signals As the only defensive player facing the entire field of play, the catcher uses finger signals to suggest which pitch should be thrown—and where. Some of the signals are fake: 2 fingers may or may not mean he's asking for a curveball. He conceals his signals by hiding his hand between his thighs and holding his mitt outside the left knee-ankle area as a shield against spying opponents.

Fielding To catch infield ground balls, the player crouches with the glove well in front of the toes (to be used like a scoop).

He watches the ball constantly until it is safely in his glove.

After catching the ball, he pulls it into his belly while preparing to throw it to the next player.

To catch a ball backhanded, the infielder crosses his left leg over his right and gets his glove close to the ground.

Outfielders play it safe when blocking ground balls: they kneel and make a trap of their legs and shoulders.

"Dugout spies are so damned clever that we have to resort to extreme measures in giving signals," says **Preston Gomez,** *3rd base coach for the California Angels. "I've often used a private set of signs for each of the regular players—about 15 of them. And on top of that, I change signs for each guy 3 or 4 times per season.*

"Sure, it can get confusing for some guys who aren't fast thinkers. I've had baserunners say to me, 'Listen, Preston, can't you just sort of nod *at the base you want to to take off for?'"*

Between 1915-1919, **Babe Ruth,** *then with the Boston Red Sox, earned one of the best left-handed pitching records ever. He twice won 23 games in a season, part of an overall total of 92 wins, 44 losses—a .626 average. His streak of 29 scoreless innings set a record that stood for 42 years.*

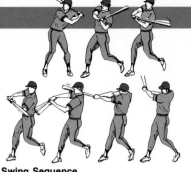

Base Stealing With his eyes glued on the pitcher (to detect any motion that would signal a pick-off attempt), the runner should be perfectly balanced—legs spread evenly, arms dangling—for a quick dash back to his original base or ahead to the next.

Double Play The shortstop has an easier play to make than the 2nd baseman, because he's moving in the direction he must throw—toward 1st base. The whole scene is in front of him. But often the incoming runner will throw up an arm or a leg while sliding in, so the shortstop should be prepared to throw while dodging flying limbs.

Pitching Delivery begins with the grip on the ball before the wind-up begins. A right-handed pitcher will then:
rock back a little onto his right foot
raise the arms above the head to set the rhythm
shift his weight forward to the foot on the pitcher's rubber by bending the knee
swing the rear leg forward to begin a kick
swivel the hips
move toward the plate, bringing the pitching arm around like a whip into the release
end with a long follow-through stride and crouch, ready to field (or avoid) a batted ball.

College men first came into the game in the pre-World War I era. Among the first were **Christy Mathewson** *(Bucknell),* **Frank Frisch** *(Fordham) and* **Eddie Collins** *(Columbia).* **George Sisler** *(Michigan) and* **Lou Gehrig** *(Columbia) followed.*

Swing Sequence
1 eye on the ball, weight on rear leg
2 swing starts with hands back of bat and hips beginning move forward
3 weight shifts to front foot
4 arms and hands throw the bat out front of the plate with the bat on a slightly downward arc
5 ball is hit with arms fully extended and wrists rolling
6 follow-through, with bat brought fully around

The greatest players have very distinctive swings. **Sadaharu Oh** of Japan hoists his front leg; **Joe DiMaggio** was known by his long, braced stride; **Pete Rose** takes a shorter 8-10″ stride.

Bat grip The knuckles on the top hand should be aligned with those of the lower hand for best bat control. The bottom hand grips the bat firmly; the top hand pinches the bat between the thumb and index finger. The bat is not thrust or stabbed at the ball, but meets it on its own impetus.

Stances
Many-time AL batting champ **Rod Carew** of the California Angels moves into 5 or 6 foot positions in the box—bugging pitchers no end. **Dave Parker** also has a variety of stances—some of which are calculated to send sparkles from Parker's earring flashing into the hurler's eyes. The various stances each have an objective:

Square or straightaway both feet are the same distance from the plate. In theory, this helps a man drive the ball back through the diamond's middle.

Open the front foot is drawn away from the plate and angled toward 3rd base by a righthanded hitter. By opening up, it is easier to observe the pitcher and pull the ball down the line.

Closed opposite of the open stance, this foot placement brings the front foot closer to the plate edge than the rear foot, enabling the batter to cover the whole plate against inside and outside pitches.

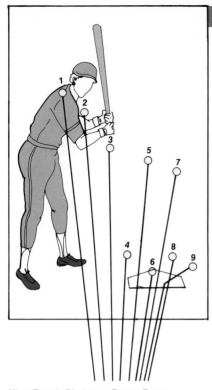

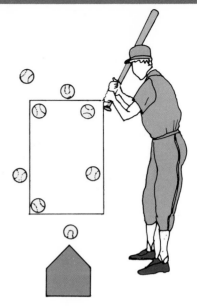

Nine Tough Pitches a Batter Faces

1 Vicious **beanball** or **knockdown** pitch, aimed at the ear area (batter must drop straight down, no time to pull back)

2 **Brushback** pitch. Aimed well inside the plate, it does not flatten the batter but prevents him from digging in on the next pitch and upsets his timing

3 **Jamming** pitch. Thrown in on the fists and to the thin, weak handle of the bat, it robs the hitter of power

4 **Inside** pitch, breaking or not breaking low on the corner of the plate at about knee level

5 **Inside** pitch thrown very hard over the plate's edge. If the ball is at waist level or above, the batter might be able to pull it to his power field

6 Sharp **curveball** breaking in on a lefthanded batter when delivered by a righthanded pitcher

7 Super **fastball** over the plate, challenging and often overpowering the batter. A ball traveling 90 to 100 mph gives the batter less time to react

8 **Slider,** a curve-fastball cross which veers left or right without much dip and on the same plane *moves over* on the hitter

9 **Low and away** (a favorite of large pitchers), catching the plate's outside corner. This pitch is the most difficult to hit, since the batter must reach for it

Strike Zone extends from the armpits to the top of the knees when batter is in a *natural stance.* It varies with the batter's height and degree of crouch.

Facts on Hitting

Pitches don't really travel the 60′6″ between the mound and the plate. Between the pitcher's forward lunge at delivery and the batter's forward stride, the true distance is closer to 55-56′.

Facing a 95-mph fastball, the batter must make the decision whether or not to swing within about ¼ sec—or when the ball is about 20′ from the plate.

Batters must meet a ball with a 2.868″ diameter no more than ½″ above or below its center to make a strong connection.

Pitchers place the ball low (inside and tight or outside and away) because low balls are harder to hit than high balls. Low deliveries mean more balls hit on the ground (to the 4 infielders) than line drives (to only 3 outfielders).

Bunting The batter stands almost facing the pitcher, with the back hand high on the bat for greater control. The ball is hit with minimal force, and usually travels relatively slowly along one of the foul lines.

A good hitter will use a bunt to surprise a 1st or 3rd baseman who is *playing deep* (standing behind his base, far from the plate), forcing the baseman to scramble in to retrieve the ball while the batter quickly takes 1st base.

Delayed Double Steal Runners at 1st and 3rd move on signal to steal 2nd and home plate. in defense, the catcher fires toward 2nd base. Depending upon the speed of the runner at 3rd, the catcher's throw is either intercepted by the 2nd baseman, who fires back to the plate

Double Play With a runner on 1st base and the ball hit to and fielded by the 2nd baseman, the classic double play begins. As the middle man on the play, the shortstop immediately breaks for 2nd, slowing up in the last 2-3 steps to be ready to catch the flip from the 2nd baseman. Taking the ball, the shortstop pivots and fires over the on-coming runner to 1st.

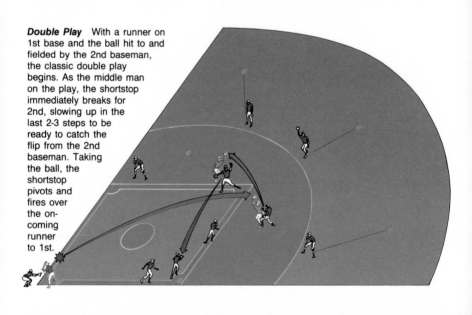

Hit-and-Run The runner on 1st races for 2nd as the pitcher's delivery begins. The 2nd baseman sticks close to his base to take the steal-preventing throw from the catcher, leaving a gaping hole between 1st and 2nd base through which the batter hits the ball.

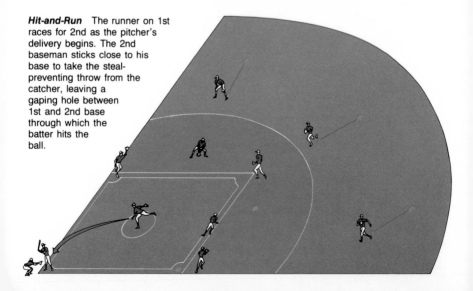

to nail the incoming runner; or the ball goes through to the shortstop who will try to put out the runner at 2nd. The main strategy is to put out the runner from 3rd base on a decoy throw, catcher to 2nd baseman and back.

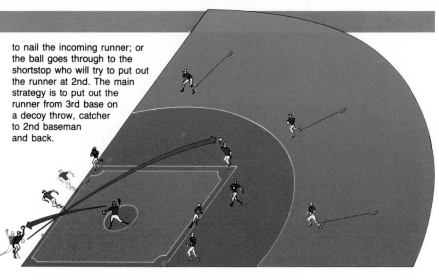

In a reverse situation, with the shortstop fielding and tossing to the 2nd baseman, the latter has a tough job. With his back to the changing runner, he must tag the base, jump over the runner and throw to 1st in a single motion. Often, the catcher runs down and backs up the 1st base-man.

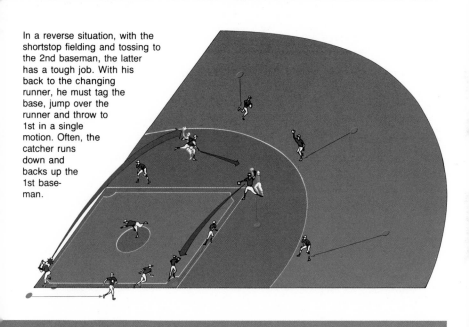

The runner, with a head start on the play, advances to 3rd. Now there are runners on 1st and 3rd, and a potential double play has been avoided.

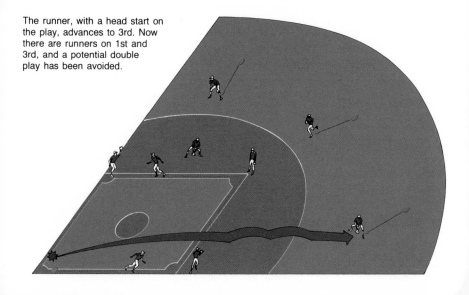

PLAYS & STRATEGIES

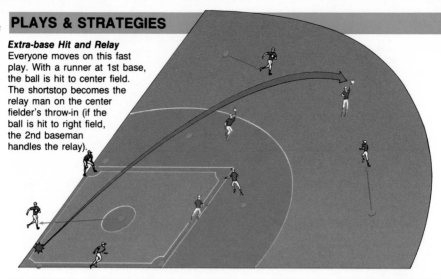

Extra-base Hit and Relay
Everyone moves on this fast play. With a runner at 1st base, the ball is hit to center field. The shortstop becomes the relay man on the center fielder's throw-in (if the ball is hit to right field, the 2nd baseman handles the relay).

Squeeze Play With a runner on 3rd, less than 2 outs and the defensive infield drawn in to protect the plate, how does a team score a runner? One way is for the batter to bunt the ball about 25' down the 3rd base line. In the *safety squeeze,* the runner at 3rd dashes for home plate as soon as the bunt is down—but no sooner—and he often beats the 3rd baseman's or the pitcher's throw to home. In the high-risk *suicide squeeze,* the runner takes off just before the pitcher throws, praying the batter lays down the bunt. If the batter fails to connect, the runner is a very dead duck.

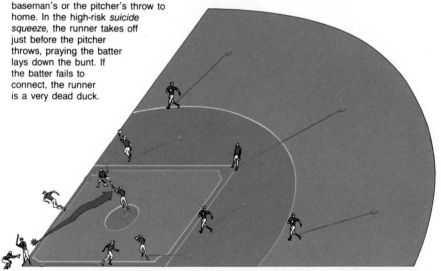

PHYSICS OF BASEBALL

A pitcher throws a ball to a batter, who hits a soaring fly that is intercepted by an alert fielder.

This simple sequence—an everyday occurrence in the game—requires each player to intuitively grasp a number of natural laws, and manipulate them to their greatest advantage.

Physics enters the game the moment the pitcher begins his wind-up on the mound. He starts by placing his body weight behind the pitching rubber, then thrusts it forward toward the plate. As he begins to deliver the pitch, he drives first with his legs, then his hips, then shoulders, arm and wrist. Then finally his fingers release the ball. This whip-like flow of momentum from the largest muscles to the smallest is an example of a biomechanical principle called ***sequential summation of movement,*** and enables him to throw the ball

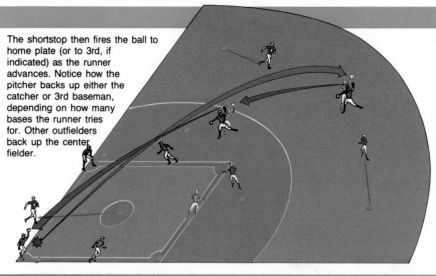

The shortstop then fires the ball to home plate (or to 3rd, if indicated) as the runner advances. Notice how the pitcher backs up either the catcher or 3rd baseman, depending on how many bases the runner tries for. Other outfielders back up the center fielder.

Two Top Gruskin *was the most deceptive pitcher who ever lived. He was signed by Duffy's All-American Irish Yankees some years ago when discovered in a bar, drinking 2 beers at once—for Two Top had 2 heads.*

Having 2 heads gave him the unique advantage of being able to watch runners on 1st and 3rd base simultaneously. Also, Two Top was a natural to pitch doubleheaders.

On the other hand, he confused his catcher by shaking off the pitch signal with one head while agreeing with the other.

His manager hesitated to approach the mound to confer with Two Top, but Gruskin didn't mind. "Three heads," he pointed out, "are better than two."

Asked where he came from, Gruskin replied, "Walla Walla." His career was a short one, because one head snored and the other couldn't get any sleep, ruining his health.

Two Top was forced to retire, but he still had a place in sports. He took a job watching tennis matches for Movietone Newsreels.

Two Top Gruskin was the beloved invention of **Ed** *Archie* **Gardner,** *star of the Duffy's Tavern hit radio show of the 1940s.*

The terminal velocity of a baseball is about 140' per second.

A few years ago, the Society for American Baseball Research, a unique organization of the games's addicts, selected the most colorful personalities of the 20th century. **Casey Stengel, Dizzy Dean** *and* **Babe Ruth** *were the 3 top choices.*

The late Stengel became a folk hero for his quaint observations, most of which have been repeated widely. But here are some lesser-known Stengelisms:
Regarding his age: *"Charley de Gaulle is older than me—and he's running a whole country."*
Upon being fired as Yankees' manager: *"Whadda I do now? Have another drink, that's what."*
On boozing ballplayers: *"My guys only had 4 beers after the game, but each beer came in a pail."*
On marriage: *"I married Edna for better or worse. But not for lunch."*
Asked where his New York Mets (a sad lot) would finish in the season's race: *"In Chicago, which is the last stop on the schedule."*
On his acumen as a player: *"I had many years that I was lousy as a ballplayer, as it is a game of skill. Did I ever tell you how I got traded for a used team bus in Kankakee IL?"*
About dentistry: *"I started out as a young fella to become a dentist. And halfway through the course whadda I find out—they don't make tools for left-handed dentists."*

95 4/9 mph

much harder than he could from a standing position.

The raised stitching on the ball enables the pitcher to use physics to control its direction of curve. The stitches create a rough surface that disturbs the paper-thin layer of air closest to the surface of the ball. This slight turbulence, called the **boundary layer,** and the airstream friction against it during its flight provide the pitcher with the means to make the ball curve, hop, rise or break. He does this by altering the *speed* and *spin* of the ball.

Speed determines when and where a pitch will curve. At low speeds the flow of air over the front of the ball will change from turbulent to smooth relatively soon, which allows the ball to begin spinning—and hence curve—earlier. At higher speeds, the flow of air over the front of the ball is more turbulent for a longer time (because of the faster air flowing over the stitches), the ball does not begin to

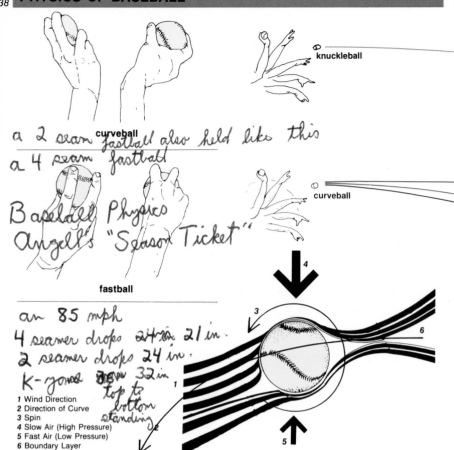

knuckleball

a 2 seam curveball *fastball also held like this*
a 4 seam *fastball*

Baseball Physics
Angell's "Season Ticket"

curveball

fastball

an 85 mph
4 seamer drops 21 in.
2 seamer drops 24 in.
K-zone 32 in.
top to bottom standing

1 Wind Direction
2 Direction of Curve
3 Spin
4 Slow Air (High Pressure)
5 Fast Air (Low Pressure)
6 Boundary Layer

spin until the turbulence gives way to a smooth flow, and the curve begins later in the pitch. Thus, the speed of the ball determines when it will begin to curve.

Spin determines how much the ball will curve, and in what direction. The ball travels in two directions: horizontally and vertically. If it is thrown sidearm, it will spin about a vertical axis (as will its boundary layer). On the side of the layer moving into the airstream, the velocity of the air moving over the ball will decrease; on the side moving with the airstream, the air velocity will increase. According to *Bernoulli's Principle,* the air pressure will be lower on the side where velocity is greater, resulting in an unbalanced force (called the *Magnus force*) that will deflect the ball to the left or right.

Of course, a pitcher rarely throws the ball on a perfectly vertical axis. Usually, he throws it at an angle that tilts the axis a little. This tilt reduces the Magnus effect, and consequently the amount of lateral deflection. A ball spinning on a vertical axis deflects right or left independent of speed or gravity. But as the axis tilts toward the horizontal, gravity will cause a downward-spinning ball to curve more or inhibit the curve of an upward-spinning ball. Tilting the axis also introduces the Bernoulli effect on upward or downward movement of the ball, causing the ball to rise or break.

To make the ball spin, a right-handed pitcher uses the wrist and finger movements described below. The movements, as well as the ball's direction, are reversed for left-handed pitchers—except for fastballs, which are thrown identically.

A **fastball** is usually thrown overhand, held on the ends of the fingers and thumb. The ball rolls off the fingers with a backward spin, and will tend to rise. A **curveball** is wedged down between the thumb and forefinger, with the wrist cocked to the left. On release, the ball is snapped down and toward the pitcher's body, and the resulting pitch drops and curves to the left. A **screwball** is thrown like a curve, except the wrist action and spin are reversed, moving *away* from the pitcher's body. It breaks down and to the right. A **slider** is thrown like a football pass, with the wrist cocked at a 90° angle, and curves slightly down and to the left. It is thrown harder than a curve, and consequently breaks less and closer to the batter. A **knuckleball** actually has little or no spin, ideally making only ¼ revolution during its trip to the plate. The lack of spin makes it aerodynamically unstable, and the raised seams create an uneven flow of air over its surface, deflecting it randomly and making it impossible for the batter to predict.

The batter sees a curveball deflecting sideways at an accelerating rate. He sees a fastball changing slightly, but approaching rapidly; a slider appears to change at the very last moment. A pitch reaches the plate in about ½ second, and since the limit of human reaction time is about ¼ second, that leaves him only ¼ second to judge the velocity, direction, curvature and rate of change of the ball's path!

To transfer momentum and power to the ball, the batter also uses sequential summation of movement. He steps forward, channeling the flow of energy through his legs, hips,

fastball rotates 14-16 times to home plate

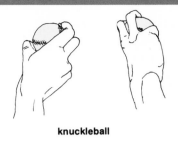

knuckleball

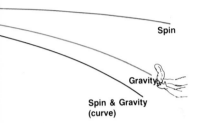

Spin

Gravity

Spin & Gravity
(curve)

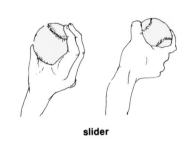

slider

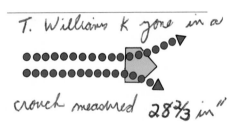

T. Williams K zone in a

crouch measured 28⅔ in"

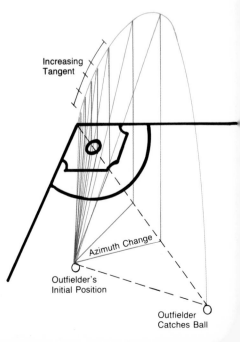

From
Williams
book on
Hitting
From
the
cover
picture

shoulders, arms and wrists to the bat. A big stride and heavy bat mean more power but less control—and control is what enables the batter to effectively use the bat's **center of percussion,** also called *the sweet spot.* This spot on the bat produces no *impulsive reaction* (vibration) at the *point of suspension* (the hands) when hit by an impulse (the ball). This allows the full force of the batter's momentum to be transmitted to the ball. This spot is usually located up from the bat's label, towards the tip, and finding it is critical: a ball landing too close to the label will cause the bat to crack; too close to the tip results in wasted power. A few millimeters high on the sweet spot may mean a fly out, and a few too low could cause a ground out.

When the ball is hit, it is compressed by the bat and momentarily deforms. As it springs off, it returns to its original shape. The amount and speed of the ball's rebound is called **elasticity,** and depends on the ball's composition. Yarn-filled baseballs have higher elasticity than air-filled tennis balls, but less than golf balls, which are filled with tightly wound rubber bands. Once the ball regains its natural shape, it behaves according to the same aerodynamic principles as a pitched ball.

The fielder uses trigonometry to catch the oncoming ball. He watches the ball rise from home plate. If it was hit directly toward him, and appears to rise at a progressively smaller rate, the fielder knows the ball was hit to the infield. But if the ball seems to ascend at a progressively greater rate, he must decide how far back he needs to move in order to meet it—a decision based on the speed at which the **tangent** of the ball's *trajectory* is increasing.

More often, the ball is hit to one side of the fielder, and this gives him the advantage of using the ball's **azimuth** to determine its destination. His 3-dimensional view of the ball's arc allows him to move with the path of the ball until the tangent has peaked and no longer appears to change. At this point, the ball will seem to fall in a straight line—directly into his glove.

Increasing
Tangent

Azimuth Change

Outfielder's
Initial Position

Outfielder
Catches Ball

Before taking the field, a pitcher-catcher battery meets to review the opponent's hitters and how best to deal with them.

But the two are also talking skulduggery—how to beat the rules and get away without getting caught.

In the old days, a 3rd baseman would grab a runner's belt to slow him down on his race for home (**John McGraw,** during his playing days with the Giants, was a master at this); a team facing some heavy hitters would freeze balls in an icebox, reducing their rate of travel; managers would plant spies in the scoreboard or outfield bleachers to steal the other team's signs. Although today's security makes cheating a more subtle art, players still try to stretch the rules:

Pitchers can *doctor* or *medicate* the ball in numerous ways, *quick-pitch* the batter before he's ready, wear a shirt adornment to annoy hitters, balk on delivery (just enough to bother the hitter, but not the umpire) or load up with enough rosin to create a small cloud of dust that obscures the ball. But altering the ball's surface is still the favorite trick.

Scuffing or *cutting* a small nick in the cowhide will cause abnormal flight—as much as 8″ of break at the plate. *Emery boards* have been used, but *sandpaper* sewn into the pitcher's glove works just as well. Raised *eyelets* on an infielder's glove or the sharp edge of a catcher's *shinguards* are also used to produced abrasions, as are small *metal flakes* imbedded in a glove. Los Angeles pitcher **Rick Honeycutt,** while with Seattle, was once ejected from a game when an umpire found a *thumb tack* under a finger bandage he wore.

Spitballs were illegalized in 1920, but it wasn't noticeable until 1968, when pitchers were banned from putting their fingers near their mouths. It's estimated that 50% of major league pitchers still grease balls with Vaseline, hair pomade or other sorts of goo; *Greaser King* **Gaylord Perry,** who retired in 1983 with 314 lifetime wins and 2 Cy Young Awards, confessed to hiding lubricants under his cap visor, inside his belt, on the back of his shirt and under the tongue of his shoe. Other players put the stuff in their sideburns, behind the earlobes, under the right armpit, on the jowls (to look like sweat), or even plant it in a nostril.

Fixed balls are so common that sometimes a pitcher will throw a batter off stride by *not* throwing one! Expecting a pitch that resembles a Wiffleball in its odd breaks, the batter gets an honest fastball. Umpires are empowered to inspect balls before each half of an inning, warn pitchers, and kick them off the field (with a 10-day suspension) if more than 1 pitched ball shows signs of tampering—but it seldom happens.

Fielders jump around on their bases to distract the batter, or move into the path of an oncoming runner just long enough to break his stride.

Runners are supposed to stay within 8′ of the basepaths, but often veer far out beyond that to obstruct a fielder shooting for a double play or to avoid being tagged out. They may let a batted ball hit them (an automatic out) to prevent a 2-out play, or slow down momentarily to block a fielder's view of an oncoming ball. These moves are foul—but aren't always called.

Batters gimmick their poles in an almost limitless number of ways. Tubes of mercury have been inserted in barrels. Metal rods are driven down the shaft. Some players *cork* their bats by drilling a hole ½″ wide and 8″ deep into the heavy end, packing in 7-8 pieces of resilient cork, and hiding the entry hole with plastic wood. **Dan Ford,** while with the Angels in 1981, was suspended for 3 days for corking his bat. Once, when **Graig Nettles** of the Yankees took a swing, his bat top broke off and out popped a half dozen rubber Super Balls, the type sold to kids. Nettles was fined.

Some club owners claim gimmicking is so rife nowadays that all bats should be X-rayed before games. Replies **Buzzie Bavasi,** California Angels, ''I'll agree to that if the owners will have their heads X-rayed, too.''

Catchers will *tip* (touch) a hitter's bat as he's swinging (although this is called *catcher's interference* and the batter may be awarded a 1st base if the catcher is caught), call a knockdown pitch, or fake a tag-out at the plate.

Base Coaches erase chalk lines in the coaching boxes with their spikes, enabling them to wander closer to see the rival catcher's signals to the pitcher. Or they'll help a runner back to a bag which he has overslid, lending a hand while they think umpires are looking elsewhere (but they're often caught).

Groundskeepers help the home team by beveling baselines to keep bunted balls in the fair zone, and *mow long* natural grass outfields to shorten the carry of balls. Such advantageous gardening is not illegal. But the San Francisco Giants were once caught watering down the 1st base area against the base-stealing Dodgers, creating a mud puddle. An umpire stopped the game and ordered it filled.

The boundaries of the football field and the basketball, tennis or squash court are governed by their respective rule books.

Baseball, too, requires limits to its playing area; but these limits are of a more malleable sort. More than any other sport (with the possible exception of golf), the character of baseball is intimately related to the borders of its landscape: the form of New York's Polo Grounds did not really affect the way football games were played there, but its effect upon the way baseball was played there was extraordinary.

There have been two major periods of ballpark construction. The first, from 1909 to 1923, witnessed the erection of 15 concrete and steel stadiums in major league cities; the second, from 1960 to the present, has seen the construction of 17 *super stadiums,* and the renovation of Yankee Stadium. The form of the first steel and concrete stadiums was determined in large part by the layout of nearby thoroughfares, and their facades typically looked out onto a city street. The super stadium, in contrast, is a freestanding object, almost universally situated in a vast parking lot.

The essence of the baseball field is the contrast between a strictly regulated *infield* area and the more loosely defined *outfield* —a 90° arc bounded by the 1st and 3rd base-lines, but otherwise of theoretically infinite extension. The first baseball game played under **Alexander Cartwright's** rules took place at Elysian Fields in Hoboken, New Jersey, on a field that was probably not much different from the setting in which most children today play their first game of ball.

The unbounded playing field encouraged a particular approach to the game. Although teams developed different strategies toward winning, the shape of the field was not a factor in those strategies since all fields were essentially the same. Baseball games were typically low-scoring affairs, because the boundless field (as well as the deader ball used in the early game) led teams to value pitching and defense, discouraged attempts at home runs, and encouraged hitters to try to place the ball between fielders—a strategy immortalized by **Wee Willie Keeler's** intent to *hit 'em where they ain't.*

In those early days, interested observers of a game would gather at convenient points around the playing field. Admission was never charged and was apparently never even considered. But the game became so popular and fan loyalties so intense that the opportunities to make money from it did not go unnoticed. The first attempt to enclose a park and capitalize on this enthusiasm was **William Cammeyer's** *Union Grounds,* built in Brooklyn in 1862. Although the enclosure movement gained steam throughout the 1860s and 1870s, it wasn't until much later that the walls became targets for hitters to drive balls over, leading to fundamental strategic changes in the game.

The first enclosed stadiums, constructed of wood, typically had a grandstand running along the 1st and 3rd baselines and behind home plate. The outfield was enclosed by a wooden fence at the outermost edge of the lot, as much as 500' from home plate—an enormous distance by today's standards, and not much different from playing in an open field. There were no bleachers. Overflow crowds would be permitted to stand in the outfield behind temporary ropes, and balls rolling into the crowd that would otherwise be home runs became ground rule doubles and triples.

Teams had very little invested in these wooden parks—which were usually built and owned by private enterpreneurs—and hence moved frequently from one park to another. As they became increasingly aware of the money-making potential of the game, many made a major capital investment in permanent parks of their own, beginning the first wave of construction of relatively permanent stadiums.

While the wooden parks were usually built on the outskirts of town to take advantage of the lower real estate prices, the new franchise-owned concrete-and-steel stadiums were typically constructed closer to the center of the city, near major transportation arteries. The first new stadiums had fields quite similar to those of the wooden ones: the outfield fences were great distances from home plate. For financial reasons, both to maximize seating capacity and increase home run production, many teams eventually constructed permanent bleachers within the confines of the stadium, moving in the fences, reducing home run distances, and changing the face of the game. In 1913, **Frank *Home Run* Baker** of the Philadelphia Athletics hit an astounding 12 home runs; by 1915, **Gavvy Cravath** of the Phillies set a record of 24 homers in smaller Baker Bowl. Fans responded enthusiastically to such heroics, and in 1919, following introduction of a livelier baseball, **Babe Ruth** hit 29 homers for the Boston Red Sox in Fenway Park, a park far more hospitable to right-handed hitters than to lefties like Ruth. After he was inexplicably sold to the Yankees, who then played in the Polo Grounds, Ruth hit 54 home runs the next year. In 1921, he upped his total to 59, and the rest is history. Ruth became a national hero, and the game of baseball has never been the same.

By 1923, 14 more stadiums of concrete and steel had opened, including:

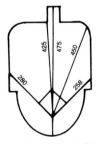

The Polo Grounds New York City. Located on Coogan's Bluff, pro baseball was played on the field from the early 1890s. The field was given its concrete and steel grandstand enclosure in 1911, following the destruction of its wooden grandstand by fire. Home of the Giants, and until 1923, the Yankees, the Polo Grounds' dimensions were peculiarly striking. The distances down the foul lines—280' to left field, 258' to right—were the shortest of any major league park in baseball history, but it was a full 475′ to straightaway center field. Pop-ups hit down the lines would become home runs, but drives hit to the power alleys or to center field that would have been homers in any other park were just long outs. It may not have always been fair, but the park played the same for everyone and stimulated countless heated discussions that did nothing if not fan the flame of baseball enthusiasm. In 22 seasons with the Giants, slugger **Mel Ott** had 511 home runs—an NL record when he retired in 1947—but in ten years playing against the Phillies when they played in Shibe Park, he never hit a home run there.

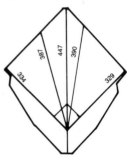

Shibe Park Philadelphia, 1909. Later known as **Connie Mack Stadium,** it was a baseball *palazzo,* the first stadium of the modern (i.e. post-1900) baseball era. The near symmetry of and great distances to the outfield walls—a reasonable 330′, more or less, down each foul line, but 390′ to the power alleys in left and right center and a staggering 447′ to dead center—bore a resemblance to the older wooden stadiums, and reflected Shibe Park's location in the gridded street plan of Philadelphia.

This article excerpted from *From Elysian Fields to Domed Stadiums: Form, Context and Character in American Baseball Parks* by **Philip H. Bess.** Originally published in *Threshold* magazine, Fall 1983. Reprinted with permission.

Players' names get mangled by fans — and some broadcast announcers. Here are some of the more difficult pronunciations among active performers:

Pitchers
Juan Eichelberger, Indians—*IKE-ul-burger*
Bobby Ojeda, Red Sox—*o-JEED-a*
Sid Monge, Phillies—*mon-jee*
Kent Tekulve, Pirates—*tuh-KULL-vee*
Ron Guidry, Yankees—*GID-ree*
Bruce Berenyi, Cincinnati—*ber-ENN-ee*
Bob Knepper, Astros—*NEPP-ur*
Jerry Reuss, Dodgers—*royce*

Infielders
Mike Scioscia, Dodgers—*SO-sha*
Luis Pujols, Astros—*POO-holds*
Lenny Faedo, Twins—*fah-A-do*
Kent Hrbek, Twins—*HER-beck*
Tony Pena, Pirates—*PAYN-yuh*
Garth Iorg, Blue Jays—*orj*
Tom Paciorek, White Sox—*puh-CHOR-eck*
Ivan DeJesus, Phillies—*de-HAY-sus*
Eddie Jurak, Red Sox—*you-rack*
Joaquin Andujar, Cardinals—*AN-do-har*
Kurt Bevacqua, Padres—*buh-VAHK-wuh*

Outfielders
Lou Piniella, Yankees—*pin-EL-uh*
Gene Tenace, Pirates—*TEN-nis*
Chris Speier, Expos—*spire*
Ron Roenicke, Mariners—*reh-NICK-ee*
Ken Landreaux, Dodgers—*LAN-droh*
Joe Lefebvre, Phillies—*luh-fay*

White Sox Park (aka **Comiskey Park**) Chicago, 1910. Now the oldest major league park in the country, it is a handsome edifice best known for its exploding scoreboard and rabid fans. Its current seating capacity of nearly 45,000 is greater than the typical park of its era, and it is still known as a pitcher's park in spite of the reduction over the years of the distance to the centerfield fence from 440′ to 404′. Original owner **Charles Comiskey** had strong feelings about keeping the field symmetrical, making it a rarity among early parks.

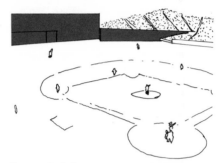

Fenway Park Boston, 1912—Widely regarded as one of the two most charming ballparks in the country (along with Wrigley Field), Fenway is noted for its perimeter deformities, particularly in center field, and for *The Wall.* This 37′-high barrier, otherwise known as the *Green Monster,* dominates left field a mere 315′ from home plate, and affects the way baseball is played in the park like nothing except an outbound wind in Wrigley Field. To left-handed pitchers, it is a nightmare; to right-handed hitters, a severe temptation. As Red Sox fans are too well aware, The Wall giveth and The Wall taketh away, but giving or taking it makes Fenway a unique baseball environment.

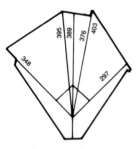

Ebbets Field Brooklyn, 1913. A cozy ballpark, just under 300′ down the right field line and less than 400′ to straightaway center field, it seated 31,500 people in two tiers. As was common in parks of this type, local merchants would rent ad space on the outfield wall, lending further to the ideosyncratic character for which Ebbets was known (Abe Stark's famous sign offered a free suit to any batter who hit it).

Wrigley Field Chicago, 1914. The only existing major league park from which Monday Night Baseball has never been televised (because it has no lights). The distances to the outfield walls in left center and right center fields are unusually short (to accommodate the outfield bleachers) and create wells down the right and left field lines that make life interesting for outfielders.

More interesting, from both an aesthetic and comic viewpoint, is the 18″ thick ivy that covers the 11′-high outfield wall, a frequent cause of lost balls and, occasionally, lost outfielders. Distances down the lines are a respectable 353′ and 355′, with 400′ to deep center. Wrigley is only 10 blocks from Lake Michigan, and winds blowing off the lake make games typically low-scoring. But a few times a year an outbound wind will cause a kind of havoc wreaked on the day in May 1979, when the Phillies beat the Cubs by a score of 23-22.

Yankee Stadium New York City, 1923. The strongest formal pressures upon the playing field were exerted by **Babe Ruth.** Left center field in Yankee Stadium was a cavern, so far from home plate (457′) that the Yankee management would one day erect monuments to Ruth, **Lou Gehrig,** manager **Miller Huggins** and Yankee president **Edward Barrow,** confident that the monuments would almost never interfere with the game being played. But to take full advantage of Ruth's extraordinary talent, the right field fence was erected a cozy 296′ down the right field line, 344′ to straightaway right, and 367′ to right center. Ruth was succeeded (much to the dismay of Red Sox fans and other Yankee-haters) by a long line of left-handed *fencebusters:* Gehrig, **Yogi Berra, Mickey Mantle, Roger Maris,** and **Reggie Jackson.**

Yankee Stadium, renovated for $100 million at public expense, still stands. Shibe Park, Forbes Field, Baker Bowl, Ebbets and the Polo Grounds have all fallen victim to the wrecker's ball, along with Cincinnati's **Crosley Field, Braves Field** in Boston, **Sportman's Park** in St. Louis, and **Griffith Stadium** in Washington DC. Of the generation of parks built betwen 1909 and 1923, only Detroit's **Tiger Stadium,** Comiskey Park, Wrigley, Fenway, and Yankee Stadium remain.

Between 1923 and 1960, only four new major league parks were built, in Cleveland (1932), Baltimore (1949), Milwaukee (1953), and Minneapolis/St. Paul (1956). But by the end of the 1950s' franchise movement, league expansion, increased team travel costs, and inflated player salaries had created a demand for new parks with greater seating capacity—a demand that continues to this day. At the same time, the cost of building and maintaining such facilities has become so great as to discourage individual franchises from building these facilities themselves. Ballpark operations per se are no longer profitable, and, once again, most ball clubs are tenants rather than landlords. Seventeen stadiums have been built since 1960, and only one—**Dodger Stadium**, opened in 1962—was financed entirely by private capital. Only three other major league teams still own their own parks, and those parks are among the oldest in baseball: Boston and Chicago in the AL, and Chicago in the NL.

The new *super stadium* is leaving a mark of its own on the game, and differs from its predecessors in three significant ways. First, the new stadiums are larger, seating as many as 60,000 people, whereas the old stadiums rarely held over 35,000. Second, the stadium of today is freestanding, isolated from the constraints imposed by tight inner-city sites. The private automobile has replaced public transportation as the major means of access, requiring proximity to multi-lane highways and acres of parking. Third, while the older parks were built exclusively for baseball teams, newer stadiums are designed as multi-purpose facilities to be used for football and soccer as well as baseball, at the insistence of the municipal and county governments who funded the projects and are interested in maximizing revenues.

These constraints have resulted in stadiums that are nearly uniform in both the shape of the playing field and the overall form. While each of the older parks had its own character, it is hard to tell **Atlanta Stadium** from **Riverfront Stadium** from **Three Rivers Stadium;** all are pure geometric forms with symmetrical playing fields nearly equal in size that provide a more or less "fair" test of hitter strength. Some of the new parks have interesting locations: **Candlestick Park** juts into San Francisco Bay; Dodger Stadium occupies high ground in Chavez Ravine, visible from freeways in downtown Los Angeles. Others distinguish themselves by building dome roofs. The granddaddy of domed stadiums is the **Houston Astrodome** (1965), a typical super stadium that is home for the Houston Astros baseball team and the Oilers football team. *Astroturf* was developed for and named after this stadium when it was discovered that the transluscent dome did not transmit enough light to grow grass. At least 6 other domes have followed, two of which (the **Kingdome** in Seattle and the **Hubert H. Humphrey Metrodome** in Minneapolis) house major league teams.

Even with the advent of the super stadium and its uniform dimensions, the game itself is still played differently on different fields. The Atlanta Braves consistently hit more home runs than the St. Louis Cardinals because Atlanta Stadium is slightly smaller than **Busch Stadium,** and also (mainly) because it is at the highest altitude of any major league park and baseballs tend to travel farther in thinner air. The Cards built a World Championship team in 1982 on speed, defense and pitching—attributes developed because they are well suited to an expansive ball park with an artificial surface on a field so hard that Busch Stadium has been referred to (not affectionately) as a *brickyard.* The Dodger pennants of '63, '65, and '66 were won by teams with the same attributes, playing in what was generally considered a pitcher's park; but in the 70s, finding themselves with a team of young power hitters, they moved the fences in 10′ and won pennants in 1974, '77, '78 and '81 that might not have been won if the fences had been left in their original position.

But these examples are hardly dramatic. Although these ball clubs have adapted themselves to the circumstances of their ballparks, the truth is that the circumstances of today's stadiums are less boldly drawn than those of an earlier generation of ballparks.

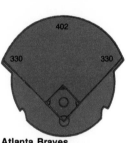

Atlanta Braves
Atlanta-Fulton County Stadium
Seats 52,194

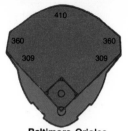

Baltimore Orioles
Baltimore Memorial Stadium
Seats 52,860

Los Angeles Dodgers
Dodger Stadium
Seats 56,000

Chicago Cubs
Wrigley Field
Seats 37,741

Boston Red Sox
Fenway Park
Seats 33,538

Montreal Expos
Olympic Stadium
Seats 60,476

Cincinnati Reds
Riverfront Stadium
Seats 51,786

California Angels (Anaheim)
Anaheim Stadium
Seats 43,250

New York Mets
Shea Stadium
Seats 55,300

Houston Astros
Astrodome
Seats 45,000

Chicago White Sox
Comiskey Park
Seats 44,492

Philadelphia Phillies
Veterans' Stadium
Seats 60,515

Cleveland Indians
Cleveland Stadium
Seats 76,713

 **National League**

Pittsburgh Pirates
Three Rivers Stadium
Seats 50,230

Detroit Tigers
Tiger Stadium
Seats 52,806

Oakland Athletics
Oakland Alameda County Coliseum
Seats 50,000

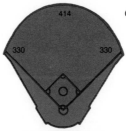

St. Louis Cardinals
Busch Memorial Stadium
Seats 50,222

Kansas City Royals
Royals Stadium
Seats 40,760

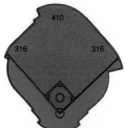

Seattle Mariners
The Kingdome
Seats 59,438

San Diego Padres
Jack Murphy Stadium
Seats 51,363

Milwaukee Brewers
Milwaukee County Stadium
Seats 53,192

Texas Rangers (Arlington)
Arlington Stadium
Seats 41,097

San Francisco Giants
Candlestick Park
Seats 58,000

Minnesota Twins
Metropolitan Stadium
Seats 45,919

Toronto Blue Jays
Exhibition Stadium
Seats 43,737

New York Yankees
Yankee Stadium
Seats 57,545

American League

Baseball has been played on every imaginable surface, from pastureland to beach sand to asphalt streets.

But major league players have always preferred closely cropped green grass, and the owners who pay the groundskeepers' salaries are increasingly enthusiastic about low-maintenance artificial turf.

Grass playing fields require a great deal of tender loving care, but they are soft to fall on, cool under summer sun, and are the ultimate playing surface that all the synthetics

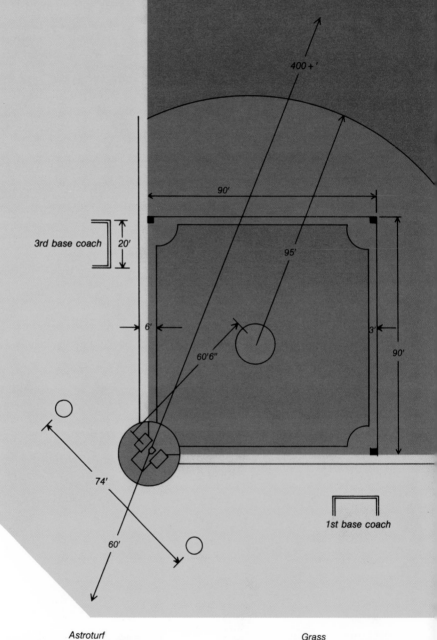

3rd base coach

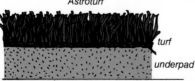

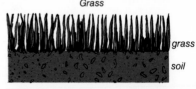

1st base coach

aspire to copy. The groundskeepers are key men in stadia that have grass fields; some have been known to move into the stadium and live there for the entire season to ensure that the turf remained a perfect, velvety green. The grass is mowed and mowed again to maintain it at a precise height, the dirt areas are constantly raked and the infield must be covered with a nylon tarp to protect it from rain (a task that requires at least 9 people).

It's no wonder that many new stadia have avoided the bother altogether and bought synthetic turf. Monsanto first introduced pro-quality nylon grass at the Astrodome (which had a hard time growing its own in the half-light of the translucent dome) in 1966, and their Astroturf products now cover the diamonds at Busch, Veteran's, Three Rivers, Riverfront and Olympic Stadiums, as well as at the Kingdome and Astrodome.

Astroturf can be laid directly over dirt surfaces (and removed if the dirt field is needed for a sport that doesn't use grass), but usually is permanently installed on an asphalt base. Seven truckloads of material are used to cover an average field. The first layer is the *underpad,* a sturdy, dense black foam rubber sheet about ¾" thick, stuck to the asphalt with a sprayed-on adhesive. The type of pad used varies with the temperature and humidity extremes of the climate. Next, the turf is unrolled over another layer of adhesive. The seams are sewn or bonded together, and the field is painted with either a permanent paint or one that can be removed if the field is to be used for different sports. Total installation time is about 2 weeks.

Early artificial turf consisted of nylon tufts that caused balls to bounce oddly and were chewed up by players' spikes, but the stuff has come a long way in 2 decades. The fibers in modern Astroturf are woven in a random pattern similar to that of real grass. Balls rebound off of it predictably—though they tend to spring higher due to the underpad. The new nylon grass will stand up to spiked shoes, and better padding makes it soft (but still somewhat abrasive) to fall on.

Degree of Bounce

Astroturf

Grass

Baseball has become a big-money sport in the 1980s.

Player salaries began a rise in the mid-70s that is nothing short of dazzling; World Series bonuses sometimes equal the yearly salaries of the men who receive them. But nothing, it seems, has escalated more than television income.

ABC and NBC's 1984 contract gives major league baseball $1.2 billion through 1989—a 400% increase over the contract that expired in 1983. Individual teams see about $7 million a year from the deal, and individual players will no doubt benefit as well.

Not that players are underpaid now: Winning a championship has become such an obsession with club owners that the average player salary for the 26 teams going into 1984 was $289,104, according to the Major League Players Association. That's a tremendous hike from 1979, when the average stood at $113,558.

But the owners' eagerness seems to prove that money won't buy everything: Only one of 1983's 6 highest paying teams, the Philadelphia Phillies, won a division championship. Here's how the highest-paying teams placed in their divisions that year:

Team	Avg Salary	1983 Rank
Yankees	$463,687	Third
Phillies	$442,165	First
Angels	$389,833	Fifth
Astros	$364,825	Third
Expos	$353,357	Third
Brewers	$352,061	Fifth

The other three championship teams, the Baltimore Orioles, Chicago White Sox and LA Dodgers, finished 11th, 12th and 13th respectively in reported gross payroll.

The biggest bonanza of all, though, belongs to World Series champions. A decade ago, bonuses came to about $25,000 for the winners and $15,000 for losers. By 1983, $65,487.70 per player went to the victorious Baltimore Orioles; the losing Philadelphia Phillies reaped $44,473.31 per man.

But is *any* player really worth that kind of money? Have salaries, multi-year contracts, bonuses and retirement benefits gone berserk? What would **Babe Ruth, Ted Williams** or **Ty Cobb** command on the modern market?

Every major league club now has at least one millionaire—and some have 4 or 5. At a million dollars per season, a player can make as much as $6000 per game—around $400 per playing minute. The main reasons for the soaring rate of player pay include:

Network TV income The player's union sees to it that members benefit from this important resource as much as owners do.

Club ticket sales and other revenue, which have risen about 10% in recent seasons.

Free agency, an innovation which frees players from team control after 6 years in the majors, and makes them independent entrepreneurs who sell their services to the highest bidder.

Pensions that are the object of envy. Not long ago, retirement pay was pretty meager, but now a player with 20 years on the job can look forward to as much as $60,000 per year for the rest of his life.

Willie Mays became the game's first $100,000-per-year player back in 1965. By 1972, **Hank Aaron** was receiving over $200,000. **Catfish Hunter** became the first player to make over $500,000 per season in 1975, **Reggie Jackson** commanded $600,000-plus in 1977, **Mike Schmidt** broke $700,000 in 1978, and **Dave Parker** hit $800,000 in 1979. By that year Angels pitcher **Nolan Ryan** had struck out a career total of 1261 batters and won 62 games in 4 seasons. Denied a 4-year contract that would bring him $1 million in the final year, Ryan signed with the Houston Astros for a reported $1 million per year.

Since then, with the rise of the baseball agent as an intimidating presence in salary negotiations, jackpots have grown even bigger. Huge Padre outfielder **Dave Winfield** accelerated the pace when he became a free agent in 1981 and signed with the Yankees in a deal that included a signing bonus of $1 million, a first-year salary of $1.4 million, and $15 million total over a 10-year period. Although Winfield will be 40 years old when the contract expires, Yankees owner **George Steinbrenner** figures he'll pay his way at the box office.

Young men with years of service ahead of them may send salary levels even higher in the future. Early in 1984, 24-year-old Dodger 2nd baseman **Steve Sax** went from $180,000 annually to a 5-year, $3 million payoff. It's possible that Sax (and many others of his generation) may more than double this income before he hangs up his spikes.

Even rookies facing their struggle to stay in the big time are well-paid. In 1975, the minimum wage for a first-year player was $16,000; by 1984, that figure had risen to $40,000.

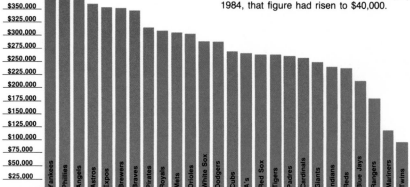

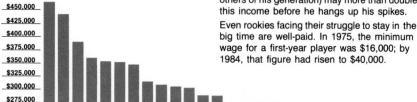

Prying a $100,000 donation out of anyone in the rock-bottom Depression days of the mid-1930s was a no-chance proposition.

Nevertheless, major league club owners raised the money without hesitation when ex-New York sportswriter **Ford C. Frick** had a grand idea: The *National Baseball Hall of Fame and Museum.*

Frick, newly named to the presidency of the National League in 1934, was browsing through the *Hall of Fame for Great Americans* in New York City one day when the thought struck him: What was good enough for Washington, Lincoln and Jefferson should also be good enough for the greatest ballplayers of the ages. He asked NL and AL owners for $100,000 (and more later) to build a spacious shrine at Cooperstown NY, the cradle of the game. Architect **Frank P. Whiting** was selected as chief designer.

Two hundred miles from Manhattan in east-central New York state, the quaint, slumbering village of Cooperstown had been known only as the birthplace of **James Fenimore Cooper,** one of the first major American novelists. But the residents saw the value in reminding the world that theirs was the city where the rough rules of primitive *town ball* were laid out well before the Civil War.

Getting the project off the ground wasn't easy. The story goes that **Babe Ruth** was among those who objected to shipping their precious belongings to "some hick town up in the woods." Later, Babe changed his mind and became one of the Hall's most ardent supporters. **Ty Cobb** didn't need to be coaxed. "It's a bang-up idea," he said. "Fans and other coyotes have stolen half of my old equipment already—and now it'll be safe."

Architect Whiting raised a 2-story building with a gable roof over white marble steps and a keystone arch bearing a baseball design. The Hall of Fame opened in 1938, and has been expanded over the years. More than 50 million people have visited it.

Beginning with the first sight a tourist notices upon entering—Babe Ruth's locker and uniform—the tour is a trip back through time, to the pioneer *New York Knickbockers Gent's Club, the Gothams, Brooklyn Excelsiors, Boston Olympics* and many other early teams.

The Baseball Writers Association of America selects the modern players and a committee of distinguished experts names the old-timers and all managers and umpires. Hall of Fame voting rules have been changed more than 20 times through the decades, but from the beginning it has required a 75% majority for a candidate to gain admission.

To be inducted into the Hall of Fame, a player generally must have played at least 10 years in the majors and be retired for at least

Baseball fans **Allan Zullo** *and* **Bruce Nash** *are establishing a* **Hall of Shame** *to commemorate the players, owners, managers and fans who gave the game its most inglorious moments. A book and museum are planned, along with induction ceremonies at the old Ebbets Field site in Brooklyn. Nominations may be sent to PO Box 6218, West Palm Beach FL 33405.*

5 years. The 5-year wait is reduced to 6 months for nominees who are over 65; deceased nominees may be elected 6 months after the date of death.

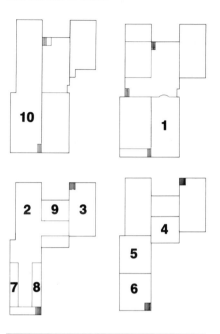

Curator's Choice

Hall of Fame curator **Ted Spencer** suggests the following as his 10 favorite highlights of the Cooperstown museum:

1
The Hall of Fame Gallery
plaques honoring the members of baseball's Hall of Fame.

2
The General History of Baseball
tracing the history of baseball from Egyptian times to the present.

3
The All-Star Game
an overview of the 51 years of the All-Star Game.

4
Babe Ruth
a 4-minute film and artifacts from his personal and professional life

5
The Old Ballparks
a tribute to parks such as Ebbets Field, Sportsman's Park and the Polo Grounds

6
History of the World Series
artifacts, records and a videotape on the 82-year history of the Series

7
Black Baseball
the history of the Negro Leagues

8
Evolution of the Uniform and Equipment

9
Baseball Cards
from 1887 to the present

10
Baseball Today
Exhibits of each current Major League Team showing the current uniform and highlighting some of today's top players.

COLLEGIATE BALL

For over a century, collegiate baseball has produced both fans and stars for the national game.

Some of the most scintillating performers in the big leagues come off campus diamonds; notable collegians include **Reggie Jackson** (Arizona State), **Steve Garvey** (Michigan State), **Dave Winfield** (Minnesota), **George Brett** and **George Foster** (El Camino College), **Goose Gossage** (Southern Colorado State), **Chris Chambliss** (UCLA), **Cecil Cooper** (Prairie View A&M) and **Fred Lynn** and **Tom Seaver** (USC). And the trend is growing: While only 40% of 1971's rookies (and no first-round choices) came from school clubs, by 1981 every one of the Houston Astros' 30 draft picks came from a college team.

Three or 4 years of NCAA play is worth one or two seasons of experience in a major league farm club, but for his extra time, a player can gain a diploma as well. **Lou Brock** of the Cardinals, who stole a record 118 bases in 1974 and had 3023 career hits, was also a prep school mathematics teacher.

Colleges act as *free farms* for the major leagues. Such ace coaches as **Rod Dedeaux** (USC), **Jim Brock** (Arizona State), **Cliff Gustavson** (Texas), **John Scolinos** (Cal Poly Pomona) and **Ron Fraser** (Florida) turn out a polished product.

The first college championship was played in 1868, when Harvard beat Yale and Princeton. The Western Conference (Big Ten) was formed in 1895 and conferences in the South and Pacific states soon followed. College-educated players soon began making it in the majors, where **Christy Mathewson** (Bucknell), **Frankie Frisch** (Fordham), **Eddie Collins** (Columbia) and **Lou Gehrig** (Columbia) proved to be quite a curiosity to the farm boys and street kids who populated the big leagues.

The College World Series began in 1947, with the California Bears taking the first title. Since then, the USC Trojans (10 championships), University of Texas (4), Arizona State (3) and Minnesota (3) have dominated the field.

Like the minor leagues, the popularity of the collegiate game has soared in the 1980s. Oklahoma State attendance figures increased a whopping 500% between 1979-1983; Arizona State, traditionally a baseball powerhouse, saw 50% more fans in the same period. And while the University of Texas team attracts over 100,000 fans a year, the box-office record belongs to the University of Miami: 163,261 fans in 1981. Due to this boom in popularity, cable networks are making big bids for the rights to college games.

AWARDS

Broadcaster Vin Scully once cracked that the national game offers more merit prizes than the Nobel Prize Committee, the Academy Awards and the French Foreign Legion combined.

Players have awards much on their minds late in the season. Aside from being assured a place in the history books, winners sometimes collect bonuses of $25,000 to $50,000 from team ownership when singled out for one of these major awards:

Most Valuable Player Two are awarded each year by the Baseball Writers' Association of America—one for the AL and one for the NL. The criteria include the entire spectrum of contributions a player can make to his team during the season. Voters look for a star's ability to hit in the clutch, his runs-batted-in, fielding efficiency, runs scored, durability and bases stolen, as well as his ability to inspire his teammates. Other prestigious MVP awards are given to the outstanding player of each year's World Series and All-Star contests.

Cy Young Award. It's named for **Denton True Cy Young**, whose 511 mound victories between 1890-1911 established an apparently unbreakable record. The award, introduced in 1956 to single out superb pitching feats, is also voted upon by the Baseball Writers Association. Steady performance over the season is a main factor. A low earned-run average, high strike-out figure, few bases-on-balls and ability to regularly beat the strongest teams also count heavily.

Gold Glove awards are sponsored by the Rawlings Co., the glove manufacturer, and voted upon by the managers and coaches of

the AL and NL. Eighteen are given per year—one to the outstanding player at each position in each league. Guys who can stop a scorching smash with elan or chase a foul pop right into a dugout or the stands are spotlighted here.

Rookie of the Year awards date to 1947. Some winners vanish from sight after a phenomenal break-in season, but the members of the Baseball Writers' Association have shown an uncanny knack for spotting raw talent—a high proportion of the young players they've singled out have gone on to glory.

Fireman of the Year awards are given by the Rolaids company to salute the relief pitchers who come in to put out the opponents' fire and save a victory. The relievers work under the heaviest pressure of any players in baseball.

Manager of the Year trophies don't always go to pilots who jet their clubs into the World Series—but it helps. In 1983, Associated Press sports editors and the Baseball Writers' Association named 2 men whose leadership produced division crowns, though not a World Series berth. In the NL, **Tommy Lasorda,** 56, brought the L.A. Dodgers through adversity to a 91-71 regular season won-lost mark and collected his third Manager of the Year trophy. The AL's **Tony LaRussa,** the quiet field marshal of the Chicago White Sox, brought his team from a late May 6th-place standing to the Chisox's first championship in 24 years.

Frick Award Established in 1978, this honor is given annually by the Hall of Fame in recognition of broadcasters who have made significant contributions to Organized Baseball—sort of an announcer's Hall of Fame. **Mel Allen, Red Barber, Bob Elson, Russ Hodges, Ernie Harwell, Vin Scully** and **Jack Brickhouse** are all members of this new but illustrious group.

The largest crowd ever assembled for an Olympic event didn't come to watch gymnasts, marathon runners, or even the opening ceremonies.

Instead, 125,000 spectators at the 1936 Berlin games turned out to watch 2 US amateur all-star teams in a demonstration of baseball—a sport that isn't even officially recognized by the International Olympic Committee, and for which the winners do not receive official Olympic recognition.

Baseball has been demonstrated at 6 Olympic meets—1904, 1912, 1936, 1952, 1956 and 1964—and though the games have been very popular, the sport has drawn little support within the Olympic movement. But with finalists from 6 countries in the first full tournament at the 1984 Games in Los Angeles, it's again possible that baseball could be an official Olympic sport for the 1988 Games in Seoul, South Korea.

A top-flight base stealer, like **Rickey Henderson** *of the Oakland A's, needs only 12 giant steps and 3 seconds to make it from one bag to the next.*

Coach **Rod Dedeaux** of the University of Southern California assembled his 20-man USA team from over 3000 amateur and collegiate ballplayers nationwide. Putting an Olympic team together requires both the cooperation of major league clubs, who may be competing for the top players needed for a winning Olympic team; and sacrifice on the part of the players, who must decide if the once-in-a-lifetime chance at an Olympic appearance is worth postponing a pro career for another season.

Although baseball is truly an international sport, with over 70 countries participating worldwide, its acceptance as an Olympic event depends on the 13 members of the IOC. Until the sport is made official, Olympic ballplayers will not march in the ceremonies or share quarters in the Olympic Village, and will receive special demonstration medals different from the ones given to regular Olympians. But the hopes are high that baseball will join the 21 other sports on the Olympic summer roster.

In 1976, Major League Baseball voted **Hank Aaron's** *715th home run as the Most Memorable Moment in Baseball.* **Babe Ruth** *was named Most Memorable Personality.*

LITTLE LEAGUE

Little League, which has produced more than 200 major league players in the last decade, is a truly universal phenomenon.

Teams come from all over the world to vie for the world's junior championship—the Caribbean, South America, the Orient, even Europe. Organized, well-equipped play for kids was first conceived by **Carl Stotz** and **Bert & George Bebble** in 1946. They started with a 3-team league in Williamsport PA (now the site of Little League Headquarters and the Hall of Fame Museum), and by the early 1960s, Little League had mushroomed into 33,000 teams and 6000 leagues in 26 countries. Now, millions of boys—and, since the 1970s, girls—cavort on diamonds under LL auspices. It's among baseball's most exciting success stories.

"When I attend a tournament," says **Johnny Bench** of the Reds, a future Hall of Famer, "I see myself at age 10 back in Oklahoma... discovering a wonderful future. I love Little League!"

Past winners of the annual World Series tournament reflect the organization's worldwide nature:

Was the game's funniest moment the time that **Casey Stengel** *doffed his cap to a booing crowd—and out flew a sparrow? Or was it the gag perpetrated by St. Louis Browns owner* **Bill Veeck** *in August of 1951?* **Bernie Ebert** *announced on the loudspeaker system, "Now batting for the Browns, number one-eighth,* **Eddie Gaedel!***" And Gaedel, a 3' 7" 65-lb midget, became the smallest batter ever to step to a major league plate. "He can't play. It's illegal!" roared umpire* **Eddie Hurley.** *"Yes, he can," countered the Browns, showing Hurley a contract signed by Gaedel. And so the smallest batter faced Detroit pitcher* **Bob Cain,** *who walked Gaedel on 4 straight pitches. Cain could hardly help it— Eddie's strike zone was only 3½".*

Winner's Home City	Year
Williamsport PA	1947
Lock Haven PA	1948
Hammonton NJ	1949
Houston TX	1950
Stamford CT	1951
Norwalk CT	1952
Birmingham AL	1953
Schenectady NY	1954
Morrisville PA	1955
Roswell NM	1956
Monterrey Mexico	1957
Monterrey Mexico	1958
Hamtramck MI	1959
Levittown PA	1960
El Cajon CA	1961
San Jose CA	1962
Granada Hills CA	1963
Staten Island NY	1964
Windsor Locks CT	1965
Houston TX	1966
Tokyo Japan	1967
Wakayama Japan	1968
Taipei Taiwan	1969
Wayne NJ	1970
Taipei Taiwan	1971
Taipei Taiwan	1972
Tainan City Taiwan	1973
Kao Hsuing Taiwan	1974
Lakewood NJ	1975
Tokyo Japan	1976
Kao Hsuing Taiwan	1977
Pin-Tung Taiwan	1978
Chia-Yi-Hsien Taiwan	1979
Hua Lian Taiwan	1980
Tai-Chung Taiwan	1981
Kirkland WA	1982
Marietta GA	1983

Women's Protective Chestguard

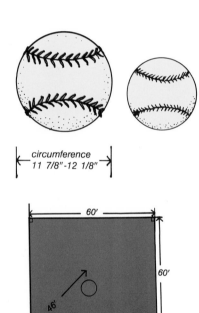

circumference
11 7/8"-12 1/8"

60'

60'

46'

People have been fascinated by stick-and-ball games since prehistoric times, and baseball is just one member of a large worldwide family of related sports.

The dozens of variations on the theme include:

Softball

Baseball's closest cousin is the most popular amateur sport in the US, with men and women of all ages participating in the more than 200,000 teams that organize under American Softball Association auspices every year.

The first softball game was played in November 1887, when **George Hancock** beat an old boxing glove around Chicago's Farragut Boat Club with a broomstick. The game spread quickly across the country, although it was played under dozens of different sets of rules until the ASA standardized the game in 1933. American soldiers took it overseas, and softball is now enjoyed by over 40 million people in 50 countries worldwide.

The game uses a larger ball but a smaller field—60' square as compared with baseball's 90'—reflecting the fact that it was originally an indoor sport. The rules were borrowed directly from baseball, with a few alterations that make it easier for the amateur to succeed. Pitching is underhanded, games run only 7 innings, and on-base runners must stay put until the batter swings at the pitch. Two kinds of softball are played: *fast-pitch,* in which the ball is flung with the speed of a baseball, making it a challenge to the hitter; and *slow-pitch,* which results in more hits and demands more of the fielders. The equipment is also different: balls are larger, measuring about 10-12" in circumference, and are rubber-coated; the bat is less tapered than a baseball bat and has a larger *sweet spot.*

Stickball

The informal and infamous street kid's game is played by as many different sets of rules as there are neighborhoods in America's eastern cities. Not even the equipment is constant: any stick will do for a bat, and the deader the projectile used as a ball, the better (to avoid breaking windows). But the game does take 2 general forms, depending on the number of players involved.

When only 2 or 3 people are playing, the playing field may resemble that of over-the-line—a triangle, with the batter standing at the apex and the pitcher in the middle. Or the batter may bounce the ball himself and hit it, while the other players act as fielders. *Bases* are defined by their distance from the plate: e.g. a ball going past the curb is a single; if it lands beyond that car parked over there it's a double; past the street light is a triple; and if it goes into the next block it's a home run. In most cases, the batter also is the umpire, though his interpretation of balls and strikes may be cause for heated discussion.

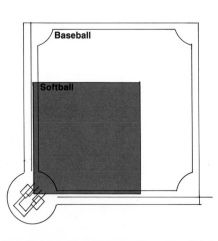

Baseball

Softball

When more players are available, the game may be set up like a regular baseball diamond, but altered to suit the confines of the site: the fire hydrant is 1st base, the manhole cover is 2nd, your little brother is 3rd and the lamp post is home plate. Dozens of big-leaguers, from **Babe Ruth** to **Hank Aaron,** hit their first homers on such makeshift diamonds—they represent the heart and soul of American baseball.

Perhaps the only major innovation in stickball in the past century is the *Wiffleball.* Designed expressly *not* to travel very far (75′ is about the limit) or do much damage, the lightweight, inexpensive Wiffle is easily controlled by young pitchers and rivals the traditional rubber *spaldeen* as the stickball of choice.

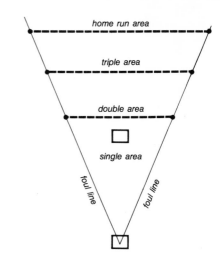

Over-the-Line

Known simply as *OTL* to devotees, this game was born on the beaches of Southern California shortly after World War II, and has become popular in the western United States wherever there are 6 people, a softball, a bat and a lot of sand. The sport is governed by the Old Mission Beach Athletic Club of San Diego, which first set down the rules and still presides over the annual OTL world championships.

Two 3-person teams play on a 60′-wide field. *The line* for which the game is named is drawn in the sand across the width of the field about 55′ from the batter, who stands at the apex of triangle *A*; the pitcher (a teammate of the batter) may stand anywhere between the batter and the line when throwing the ball. Behind the line, the fair zone extends for an undetermined but substantial distance, and is covered by fielders of the opposing team. Hits are scored when a fly ball hit into fair territory is missed by fielders (no gloves are allowed), when a fielder touches and drops a batted ball, or when a fielder crosses the line while in pursuit of a ball. A home run is scored when the ball travels past all 3 fielders without being touched. Three hits must be made in a single inning before one run can be counted; each subsequent hit in that inning counts as one run.

The batter is out when he hits 2 foul balls, a fly ball that is subsequently caught, or a ball that lands on one of the lines; misses one strike; or if the pitcher crosses the line into the opponent's territory. Like baseball, there are 3 outs to the inning; 5 innings constitute a game.

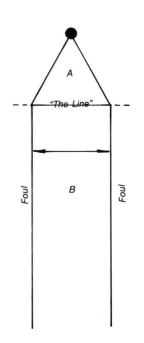

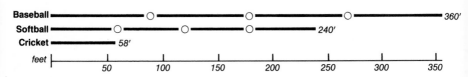

Cricket

The earliest ancestor of baseball, cricket has been the game of choice for gentlemen of the British Empire for almost 3 centuries. The Marylebone Cricket Club, founded in 1787, is cricket's governing body, and its laws specify every aspect of the sport from the way the grounds are maintained (mowed very short and never watered the day of a match) to the

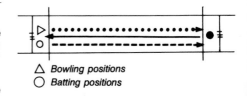

△ *Bowling positions*
○ *Batting positions*

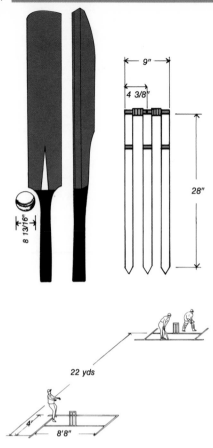

match) to the clothes the players wear (white or cream shirts and long pants).

The cricket field, called a *pitch,* is 22' long and 10' wide. At each end stands a *wicket,* comprising 3 *stumps* (uprights) on which two *bails* (small wood pieces) are gently balanced. At one end of the pitch stands a *bowler* (pitcher), who attempts to knock the bails off the far wicket with the ball; a runner from the batsman's team; and an umpire. At the other end is the batsman, who stands in front of the wicket and defends it by hitting the ball away; and the *wicket keeper,* a member of the bowler's team, who tries to catch the bowler's ball and use it to knock down the wicket.

A run is scored when the batsman hits the ball and runs to the opposite end of the pitch, while his teammate on the bowler's end runs the opposite way—the two players simply switch ends. If both make it to their respective goals, the team is awarded one point. Outs are made when the bowler or wicket keeper succeeds in knocking the bails off one of the wickets with the ball before the runners reach their goals, or (as in baseball) when a fly ball is caught by one of the fielders who are scattered in the area around the pitch.

The game is divided into *overs* and *innings.* An over ends when the bowler has thrown the ball 7 times; teams trade sides of the playing field after each over. An innings (there's an *s* on the end) is completed when every player on both 11-man teams has been put out. Most games consist of only 1 or 2 innings, but since teams trade sides frequently and numerous details regarding the field and equipment must be attended to, cricket matches commonly last for 2 or 3 days.

THE MINORS

Down on the farm they're growing tomorrow's crop of headliners. America's minor leagues—from Class AAA to rookie—are where it all begins for most of the players who make it to the big time.

Reggie Jackson for example, began his career in the Northwestern League's Lewiston ID franchise. **George Brett** broke in at Oneonta on the New York-Pennsylvania circuit. **Mike Schmidt** honed his skills on the Reading PA team of the Eastern League. **Steve Garvey** played at Ogden UT with the Pioneer League. **Goose Gossage** started with Sarasota FL in the Gulf Coast loop.

At one time, almost 60 minor leagues from Class AAA to Class D operated from coast to coast. But television brought major league ball into even the smallest communities by the late 1950s, cutting fan support for local teams. Only 16 leagues survived, and their member teams are either affiliated with AL or NL teams or owned outright by them. These leagues are divided into 3 categories:

Class AAA—One step below the majors, this category includes the American Association, International League and Pacific Coast League.
Class AA—The Eastern, Southern and Texas leagues.

Class A—California, Carolina, Florida State, Midwest, South Atlantic, New York-Pennsylvania and Northwest leagues.
Rookie—Formerly called Class B, C and D leagues, they include the Appalachian, Gulf Coast and Pioneer circuits, among others.

The minors are enjoying a coast-to-coast renaissance in the 1980s. The Eastern League has enjoyed an 80% increase in attendance, and for the first time, one team's season attendance figures exceeded the magic million mark. The American Association's Louisville Redbirds, who had pulled a sensational 868,418 customers in 1982, drew 1,052,438 in 1983—more fans than 3 major league teams (Cleveland, Seattle and Minnesota) drew during the same season! In fact, Louisville attracted an average of 16,191 people per playing date—a number that 5 big league teams couldn't match. Much of the credit for the Redbirds' incredible success belongs to owner **A. Red Smith**, who attracts crowds with a Disneyland-like concession set-up, a beer garden, a concourse with bands and $1 tickets on special courtesy nights.

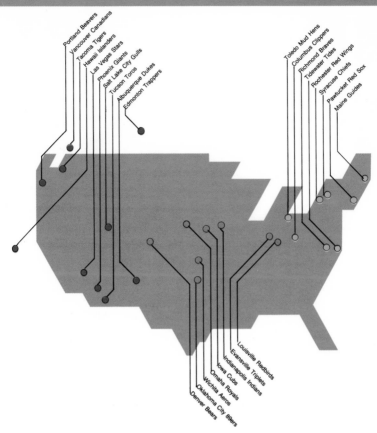

Class AAA teams that serve as top farm clubs for the majors are:

Pawtucket RI	Boston Red Sox	**Syracuse NY**	Toronto Blue Jays
Rochester NY	Baltimore Orioles	**Richmond VA**	Atlanta Braves
Edmonton Canada	California Angels	**Des Moines IA**	Chicago Cubs
Denver CO	Chicago White Sox	**Indianapolis IN**	Montreal Expos
Evansville IN	Detroit Tigers	**Tuscon AZ**	Houston Astros
Old Orchard Beach ME	Cleveland Indians	**Albuquerque NM**	Los Angeles Dodgers
Omaha NB	Kansas City Royals	**Wichita KS**	Cincinnati Reds
Vancouver BC	Milwaukee Brewers	**Tidewater VA**	New York Mets
Toledo OH	Minnesota Twins	**Portland OR**	Philadelphia Phillies
Columbus OH	New York Yankees	**Hawaii**	Pittsburgh Pirates
Tacoma WA	Oakland A's	**Louisville KY**	St. Louis Cardinals
Salt Lake City UT	Seattle Mariners	**Las Vegas NV**	San Diego Padres
Oklahoma City OK	Texas Rangers	**Phoenix AZ**	San Francisco Giants

Words & Music

It's possible that baseball has been more celebrated in song and story than any other sport. Here are the origins of 3 of the most popular verses:

Take Me Out To The Ball Game *Broadway actor-composer* **Jack Norworth** *wrote the words to baseball's immortal anthem during a trolley trip to a game in 1905. "By the time I'd got to the ballpark, I'd finished it," Norworth later said. He took his lyrics to* **Albert von Tilzer,** *a songwriter, who added the melody.* **Nora Bayes,** *a popular actress (who also happened to be Norworth's wife) introduced the song to her audience one night in 1906. It proved to be such a hit that 80 years later fans still stand and sing it during the 7th-inning stretch.*

Casey At The Bat *During a visit to San Francisco in 1888, Harvard Student* **Ernest L. Thayer** *handed the editor of the local* Examiner *a 12-stanza poem he'd written about a fearsome slugger named Casey. The editor published it in the 3 June edition, with the subtitle* A Ballad To The Republic.

Who's On First? *The origin of this imperishable* **Abbott & Costello** *routine is shrouded in mystery. Some say that a script was written, but Bud Abbott once said that "Lou and I sort of made it up as we went along."*

Baseball has been Japan's national game almost as long as it has been America's.

Catholic missionary **Horace Wilson** assembled teams for the first game in 1869, shortly after Japan opened its doors to the West; the official rules were translated into Japanese in 1877.

US All-Star team visits before and after World War II made **Babe Ruth, Lou Gehrig** and **Joe DiMaggio** Japanese heroes, and led to the establishment of a professional league in 1936. Despite the animosities of World War II, Oriental enthusiasm for the game continued unabated. Recently, annual exhibition games have been held between the Japanese and US World Series champions, and they may set the stage for a truly *World* Series in the near future.

The modern game is soaked with *komochi* (tradition). Each year more than 13 million fans come out to Japan's major league ballparks, including Tokyo's *Jingu Stadium,* Nagoya's *Chunichi Stadium,* Osaka's *Nishinomiya Stadium,* and *Hiroshima Stadium.* The Japan Series—the country's championship playoff—attracts 60,000 or more fans, who observe time-honored rituals that American spectators would find quite odd.

In Japan, *players bow with respect to umpires.* When notorious ump-hater **Leo Durocher** first toured Japan with his New York Giants, he protested loudly at this gesture of deference—but, to his everlasting shock, wound up doing it anyway. Yet the umpire's word is not law in the field, and it is not uncommon for officials to change their minds to placate an irate manager.

After striking out, the Japanese ballplayer *smiles politely* and returns quietly to the bench. Replaced pitchers, however, go to the bullpen and keep throwing until they meet the approval of the spectators.

Tie games are common in Japan's Central and Pacific Leagues because of a tough 10pm curfew.

Foul balls that land in the stands are promptly returned to the umpire.

Players don't seek *personal glory,* preferring the concept of *wa,* total dedication to the team at a sacrifice of the self. Because of this philosophy, holding out for more money as American players do would be considered selfish and uncouth.

Teams are owned by major corporations instead of owing their allegiance to cities. Hence, one of the 4 Osaka-based teams is known as the Hanshin Tigers, since it is owned by the Hanshin Electric Railway Corp; the Chunichi Dragons, Nagoya's home team, are named after a newspaper chain. Dominating the game there, as the New York Yankees have done here from time to time, are the Yomiuri Giants of Tokyo, owned by media conglomerate Yomiuri Shimbun (the team is an exception to the above rule: they are generally called the Tokyo Giants). They once won 19 championships in 23 seasons— 9 of them in a row. The 12 major league teams each play about 130 games per season.

Food at a Japanese baseball game includes the requisite American hot dogs and peanuts—but rice, sushi, fish and vegetable dishes are also sold in styrofoam containers. Like Western fans, the Japanese enjoy their meal with a beer or a Coke.

Despite the differences, once the game begins the American fan feels immediately at home. The same rule book is used, and despite the strong team identity, Japanese stars are even more revered than their counterparts back home. All-time home run king (with over 800 HRs) **Sadaharu Oh** needed a bodyguard and was paid nearly $250,000 per season (about the same as top US players) during his prime in the mid-70s. Other fan favorites include **Katsuya Nomura,** infielder **Shigeo Nagashima** and lefthanded pitcher **Masaichi Kaneda.** Although there is demand in the US for players of their quality, only one Japanese player—**Masanori Murakami,** a left-handed pitcher with the San Francisco Giants in the '60s—has played in the American majors. Why would one go to a country where they boo the umps and spit tobacco on the dugout floor?

But many American major league players have migrated to Japan to continue their careers. Japanese teams are permitted to include no more than 2 *gaijin* (foreign) players on the roster, and will pay up to $100,000 per season for top talent. Americans **Orlando Cepeda, Don Newcombe, Daryl Spencer, Clete Boyer, Wes Parker** and **Jim Lefebvre** have made the crossing; **Warren Cromartie,** formerly of the Expos, commanded a high price when he made the move. Though the US imports often establish long and happy careers (or come back reeling from culture shock), only pitcher-turned-1st baseman Newcombe has been successful enough to make the Japanese All-Star team.

Despite governmental attempts during World War II to originate baseball terms based in the Japanese language, most are still derived from English:

basuboru baseball
pichah pitcher
kyachah catcher
hitto a hit
foul foul
safu safe
fasto basu first base
banto bunt
sutoraiku strike
homma (or sayonara) home run
outo out
pooray boru! play ball!

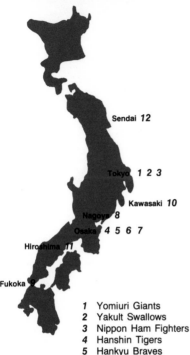

Sendai **12**

Tokyo **1 2 3**

Kawasaki **10**

Nagoya **8**

Osaka **4 5 6 7**

Hiroshima **11**

Fukoka **9**

1 Yomiuri Giants
2 Yakult Swallows
3 Nippon Ham Fighters
4 Hanshin Tigers
5 Hankyu Braves
6 Nankai Hawks
7 Kintetsu Buffalos
8 Chunichi Dragons
9 Taiheiyo Club Lions
10 Taiyo Whales
11 Hiroshima Toyo Carp
12 Lotte Orions

LATIN AMERICAN BALL

United States

Japan

Cuba

Mexico

Dominican Republic

Central and South Americans share their North American neighbors' enthusiasm for baseball.

Venezuela, Colombia, Mexico, and the Caribbean countries (particularly the Dominican Republic and Puerto Rico) are populated with millions of die-hard baseball fans, and produce some of the game's biggest stars.

For decades, Cuba was the heart and soul of Latin American baseball, and hundreds of Cubans came to the US mainland to make it in the majors. But the flow of top-quality talent ceased abruptly in the early '60s when Fidel Castro assumed power, and now the

biggest player-exporting nation by far is the Dominican Republic. Over 150 major-leaguers, including **Juan Marichal,** the **Alou** brothers—**Felipe, Matty** and **Jesus**—**Pedro Guerrero, Tony Pena** and **Cesar Cedeno** have come from an island only one-third the size of Florida. There may be 3 dozen Dominican players on major league rosters in an average year. A close second (providing about 30 active players each season) is Puerto Rico, home territory of **Orlando Cepeda, Ruben Gomez, Candy Maldonado,**

Roberto Clemente

Ivan de Jesus, Tony Aviles and the late, great **Roberto Clemente.** Venezuela also produces its share of stars—the Phillies' **Manny Trillo** and Cincinnati star shortstop **Dave Concepcion**—and Mexico's 5 summer and 2 winter leagues, long considered an extension of the US minor leagues, are now gaining in prestige with the success of **Fernando Valenzuela.** Venezuela and Mexico each supply nearly a dozen players to the majors yearly.

In 1984, a total of 110 Latin players were working in the US big leagues, and the numbers will doubtless increase in the decade ahead as US scouts become more aggressive. Many countries reinforce the Latin American connection by hosting US pro teams during

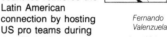

Fernando Valenzuela

the Winter Leagues season. A major league manager may contract with a club in Venezuela or Puerto Rico to send a few of his hottest rookies for an off-season workout that polishes the new recruits; ambitious minor league managers (who once included **Sparky Anderson** and **Tom Lasorda**) also gain experience outside the US. In exchange for their hospitality, the home teams receive the services of near-pro quality managers and players, plus financial benefits that enable them to build their own clubs—but there is a high risk that a few local players will end up returning with the visitors to play in the US

Despite close ties with *Los Estados Unidos,* baseball games in Latin countries take on a flair of their own. Bookies and street vendors may be permitted to work the stadium aisles; arguments between major-league caliber players and less knowlegeable local umpires are heated and frequent. Native foods are served: in Mexico, the *taco* (meat, cheese and vegetables wrapped in a *tortilla* and deep fried) is enjoyed with the local beer; in the Caribbean, they might eat *tostones* (fried plantain fritters) and drink *maltas* (a grain-based soft drink).

*Over 80 major league players have had at least one son who followed in their footsteps; 5 players (including the Hall of Famer **George Sisler**) have sent 2 sons to the majors.*

As professional baseball moves into its second century, many of its most important records are likely to fall.

The game's emphasis on statistics makes it easy to quantify the achievements of its heroes. Here are 9 of baseball's most impressive feats, and the stars who accomplished them:

.400 season batting average Despite the lively ball and synthetic turf used in the modern game, no one has been able to maintain a .400 batting average for an entire season since the Red Sox' **Ted Williams,** who hit .407 in 1953. Williams and .401 hitter **Bill Terry** of the 1930 New York Giants have been the only players in over half a century to reach this figure.

Between 1900 and 1925, swinging at a much deader ball on slow dirt fields, 6 men topped .400. Two of them—**Ty Cobb** and **Rogers Hornsby**—did it 3 times. The entire group includes:

Nap Lajoie .422, 1901
Joe Jackson .408, 1911
Ty Cobb .420, 1911; .410, 1912; .401, 1922
George Sisler .407, 1920; .420, 1922

Harry Heilmann .403, 1923
Ted Williams .406, 1941
Rogers Hornsby .401, 1922; .424, 1924; .403, 1925
Bill Terry .401, 1930

3000 Career Hits While the majority of .400 hitters were old-timers, 8 of the 14 men who made a career total of 3000 hits played between 1940-1980, which reflects the staying power and immense ability of today's players. This feat eluded towering hitters **Rogers Hornsby** (2930), **Babe Ruth** (2873) and **Al Simmons** (2927), but among recent players, **Pete Rose** has proven himself the equal of **Ty Cobb,** who was for decades the only 4000-hit man.

Ty Cobb	4191
Pete Rose	+4000
Hank Aaron	3771
Stan Musial	3630
Tris Speaker	3515
Honus Wagner	3430
Carl Yastrzemski	3419
Eddie Collins	3311
Willie Mays	3283
Nap Lajoie	3251
Paul Waner	3152
Lou Brock	3023
Al Kaline	3007
Roberto Clemete	3000

500 Career Home Runs The mighty **Babe Ruth** stood at the top of this dozen-member group until 9:07pm 8 April 1974, when **Henry Aaron** unloaded his historic 715th home run. Ruth's 714-home-run record had been considered unassailable, but the quiet man from Mobile AL chipped away at it—and it's possible that his feat may never be equaled by an American player (**Sadaharu Oh** of Japan holds the ultimate world record with over 800 home runs). **Reggie Jackson** will unquestionably complete his career as a member of the 500-homer group.

Hank Aaron   *Mickey Mantle*

Hank Aaron	755
Babe Ruth	714
Willie Mays	660
Frank Robinson	586
Harmon Killebrew	573
Mickey Mantle	536
Jimmy Foxx	534
Ted Williams	521
Willie McCovey	521
Eddie Mathews	512
Ernie Banks	512
Mel Ott	511

50 Home Runs in a Season Only 10 players in the history of the game have achieved this goal, which demands that hitters knock out a homer about once every 10-12 times at bat. **Babe Ruth** did it first in '21 (and again 3 more times in his career); his 60-run mark stood until 1961, when **Roger Maris** averaged a home run every 9.6 times at bat for a total of 61 HRs. Maris' record is controversial because he played a 162-game schedule compared to 154 for the Babe—but Maris reached his 60th run on his 684th appearance at the plate, while Ruth reached the same number in his 687th appearance.

Babe Ruth

Roger Maris	1961	61
Babe Ruth	1927	60
Babe Ruth	1921	59
Hank Greenberg	1938	58
Jimmie Foxx	1932	58
Hack Wilson	1930	56
Babe Ruth	1920	54
Mickey Mantle	1961	54

Ty Cobb

Babe Ruth	1928	54
Ralph Kiner	1949	54
Mickey Mantle	1956	52
Willie Mays	1965	52
George Foster	1977	52
Ralph Kiner	1947	51
Johnny Mize	1947	51
Willie Mays	1955	51
Jimmie Foxx	1938	50

300 Career Pitching Victories Since the turn of the century, only 10 pitchers have won 300 games in a career. **Steve Carlton** and **Gaylord Perry,** who made the grade in 1983 and '82 respectively, are the first pitchers to reach 300 since **Early Wynn** did it in 1931; **Phil Niekro, Jim Palmer** and **Don Sutton** are not far behind. But the all-time leader of this pack is **Denton True Cy Young,** an early-century marvel who lasted 21 years and won a stupendous 511 games.

Cy Young

Cy Young	511	.620
Walter Johnson	416	.599
Christy Mathewson	373	.665
Grover Alexander	373	.642
Warren Spahn	363	.597
Gaylord Perry	314	.542
Edward Plank	305	.628
Robert Grove	300	.680
Early Wynn	300	.554
Steve Carlton	300	.600

3000 Career Strikeouts The most elite pitchers' group has only 8 members, led by Steve Carlton with 3709. Phil Niekro will likely be #9. The entire roster includes:

Walter Johnson

Steve Carlton	3709
Nolan Ryan	3677
Gaylord Perry	3534
Walter Johnson	3508
Tom Seaver	3272
Ferguson Jenkins	3192
Bob Gibson	3117
Don Sutton	3065

50 Career Shutouts Walter Johnson's record of 110 shutouts will probably stand forever, since nobody today works anything close to the 4500 or more career innings pitched by the old-timers who dominate this category. But the 50-shutout mark is still attainable, as **Nolan Ryan, Steve Carlton** and (soon) **Ferguson Jenkins** are proving.

Christy Mathewson

Walter Johnson	110
Grover Alexander	90
Christy Mathewson	83
Cy Young	77
Edward Plank	64
Warren Spahn	63
Bob Gibson	56
Tom Seaver	56
Don Sutton	56
Steve Carlton	55
Gaylord Perry	53
Jim Palmer	53
Juan Marichal	52
Nolan Ryan	52
Mordecai Brown	50

700 Career Steals Only 5 players ever reached this mark. **Ty Cobb,** who played 1905-28, may have been the best burglar of all: even though he lacked today's lightweight shoes and smooth runways, he ran up 892 steals. But the record belongs to **Lou Brock** of St. Louis, who led the majors in stealing for 8 seasons, with a high of 118 steals in 1974. That broke **Maury Wills'** 1962 mark of 104, when Wills often played with bloody thighs and chipped anklebones. Oakland's **Rickey Henderson** is the next great *King of Thieves,* with a shot at an unprecedented 3 consecutive 100-steal seasons.

Lou Brock	938
Ty Cobb	892
Eddie Collins	743
Max Carey	738
Honus Wagner	720

1900 Career RBIs This is the fraternity of superb clutch hitters, connecting with men on base when it counts. Only 3 of its 7 members performed after World War II: **Stan Musial, Willie Mays** and **Henry Aaron. Lou Gehrig,** who ranks third on this list, may well have become the all-time RBI leader, but his battle against ALS (amyotropic lateral sclerosis) cut both his life and his career tragically short.

Hank Aaron	2297
Babe Ruth	2204
Lou Gehrig	1990
Ty Cobb	1960
Stan Musial	1951
Jimmy Foxx	1921
Willie Mays	1903

Two of the strangest trades in baseball history: **Cy Young** *(later to become the winningest of all pitchers) was swapped to Cleveland for a suit of clothes; Dallas sent hurler* **Joe Martina** *to New Orleans for 2 barrels of oysters.*

The baseball record books would probably look very different if such players as Josh Gibson, Joe Williams, Satchel Paige, Oscar Charleston, *Cool Papa* Bell and Spottswood Poles had been permitted to join the all-white majors between 1889-1947.

In fact, dozens of extraordinary performers were denied the opportunity to make their mark on the game after the baseball color barrier was raised in 1887.

Moses Fleetwood Walker was the first of several black players who entered the majors during the early 1880s, and their presence became an issue almost immediately. **Cap Anson,** who wielded considerable power as the leader of the Chicago White Stockings, was especially vocal and refused to take the field against any nonwhite team. In 1887, the league directors bowed to Anson and agreed to sign no more contracts with black players; by 1890, segregation was complete.

Though some players continued to play in the majors by passing themselves off as Cuban or Indian, others joined the Southern League of Colored Base Ballists, founded in 1886, or one of the number of independent leagues that followed. It wasn't until 1920 that the first true Negro League, the Negro National League, was founded by **Rube Foster;** the Negro American League followed in 1937. Many of the teams rented stadiums from white teams who were away on road trips, and exhibition games between white major league and Negro League teams were frequent. Although a black World Series was played

from 1924, the biggest spectacle of Negro League ball was the East-West Classic, first held in 1933. Families from all over the country came to Chicago for this all-star extravaganza, which regularly featured such legendary players as **Walter *Buck* Leonard,** a *black Lou Gehrig* whose batting average was almost .400; **John Beckwith,** a huge man known for his powerful hitting and outstanding speed; **Jim *Cool Papa* Bell,** who was so fast around the bases that **Jesse Owens** reportedly refused to race him; and *Smokey Joe* **Williams,** the pitcher who mowed down **Ty Cobb** and **Tris Speaker** in exhibitions and beat **Christy Mathewson** and **Grover Cleveland Alexander** in head-on confrontations.

The immense talent and popularity of the Negro League players was not lost on Brooklyn Dodgers owner **Branch Rickey,** who announced on 28 October 1945 that he had signed a young shortstop named **Jackie Robinson.** Black spectators turned out by the thousands to see Robinson and the other players who soon followed him into the majors. Four years later, the East-West Classic drew its final crowd; within a decade professional Negro Leagues nationwide collapsed as their stars and their fans headed for the newly-integrated major league teams.

HISTORY OF PROFESSIONAL BASEBALL

Americans were whacking at homemade twine balls with bats constructed by local wood-turners in the nation's earliest days, but the origins of baseball are as old as man.

Egyptian tomb carvings more than 5000 years old show batting contests using balls that were probably made of packed papyrus. Moors picked up stick-and-ball games from

Arab tribes who'd seen the Egyptians in action, and brought them to Spain and France somewhere around the 11th century. Balls were kicked (from which came soccer football), hit with a club (from which came golf) or swatted with a pole or stick (cricket).

The British developed a variation which was the first recognizable ancestor of US baseball. The pitcher tried to slip the ball past a stick-holder to hit a stool behind him. When more wooden stools were added, bases evolved. In time a kid's game called *feeder* or *rounders* was developed, in which players ran around wooden posts stuck in the ground. English colonists brought rounders to the new land, where it became known in New England as *base* or *goal* ball. The *1834 Book Of Sports,* the first baseball publication in this country, shows baseposts laid out in the form of a diamond.

For years, **Abner Doubleday,** a bewhiskered Civil War general, was held by Organized Baseball to be the "inventor" of baseball (never mind the Egyptians or British). But after extensive research, old Abner was discredited. He contributed a good deal to the game from 1839 onward; however, **Alexander Cartwright,** a New York fireman who became a professional surveyor, actually set down the formal rules and field layout in 1845 to end the chaos that overwhelmed the sport.

Under the primitive Town Ball rules, any number could play. No fixed game-time limit existed. Teams scored *aces* (runs) until exhaustion set in, then called it a day. Baserunners could be put out by *plugging* (hitting) them with a thrown ball. Diamond sizes varied from town to town.

Cartwright decreed that whichever team first scored 21 runs was the winner. Canvas bases were installed, with a flat iron disc for home plate. Baserunners had to be put out by a fielder tagging them—plugging the runner was forbidden. Other innovations included the 3-strike out (earlier, 4 or more strikes were allowed), 3 outs to the inning, and the rules concerning foul balls.

Cartwright retained the traditional pitching distance of 45', as well as the requirement that balls be delivered underhand (overhand pitching didn't arrive until 1884). And he allowed an advance of only one base if the ball was hit out of the infield. But his real design masterpiece was the distance between bases. Surveyor Cartwright somehow realized that precisely 90' between bases was ideal. This was such a stroke of genius that the distance hasn't changed an inch in all the years since. Some historians think that he picked that figure because in circling the bases a runner travels 360'—the number of degrees in a circle. Others believe he just got lucky. At any rate, today we wouldn't have the nip-and-tuck plays between the runner and the throw to 1st base, or the close plays on base steals, if the bags had been set at some other distance. "We learned the lesson" says one modern researcher, "that human foot speed and the strength of fielders' arms weren't much different back then than they are now."

Adds **Jimmie Reese** of the California Angels, "The guy had to know something. At 90' a batter is retired on an ordinary bounder. But if he hits it deep to 3rd, short or even 2nd base, or if the fielders are a shade slow in handling the ball, he can beat out the throw. Cartwright did a beautiful thing."

Many of the changes in the game since Cartwright resulted from improvements in the equipment. Until 1875, pros played barehanded and frequently shattered fingers. They had no protective head or body equipment of any kind. Uniforms were gaudy and peculiar. Some traveling *exhibition* clubs wore clownish outfits colored by position— green for outfielders, blue for infielders. In 1880 baggy bloomer pants were the rage. Shirts were laced to the throat with drawstrings to keep out dirt. Collars flared up to shield the neck, and caps were short-billed. Thick mustaches, sideburns and bristling beards were part of a man's fierce appearance.

Improvement in equipment progressed rapidly through the 1800s:

1860s First costumers are *Horsman's Base Ball Emporium* and *Bassler the Hatter* of New York (they also make coats for **Prince Albert** and the silk tophats worn by umpires).

1869 First fully uniformed club, New York Knickerbockers, decked out in blue and white.

1875 Introduction of the catcher's mask by **Jim Tyng** of Boston. An invention of his Harvard teammate **Fred Thayer,** it reduces players' demand for dentists and bonesetters.

1876 First fielder's glove (no webbing, just a scrap of leather) is worn by **Charles Waite,** 1st baseman/outfielder for St. Louis.

1877 First player to wear glasses, Boston pitcher **Bill White.** No non-pitcher dared to wear specs until 1921.

1883 First numbered uniforms worn by the Cincinnati Red Stockings.

1884 First custom-made bat, by Louisville KY woodturner **John Hillerich,** is made for noted slugger **Pete Browning.** Hillerich founded Hillerich & Bradsby, which still manufactures the million-selling Louisville Slugger.

1887 Introduction of pants with sliding pad inserts, a boon for base stealers.

1885 First use of chest protectors by catchers and umpires.

1887 Introduction of webbing between the thumb and first finger of gloves, causing an outcry over *these disgusting huge hand coverings.* By today's standards, the old gloves were ridiculous affairs with almost no padding.

1895 Many outfield fences are painted dark colors—**Jimmy *Bug* Holliday** of Cincinnati fell from a .383 average to .301 and claimed he couldn't see the ball against white fence ads.

1896 First major training aid, a mechanical robot pitcher, is invented by **Professor Charles H. Hinton** of Princeton. The gadget fires a ball through a tube by way of an exploding cartridge.

1900 New 5-sided home plate designed, replacing the square plate and giving the pitcher a straight line down which to aim.

1907 First shinguards for catchers are the bright idea of Irish-born **Roger *Duke of Tralee* Bresnahan** of New York Giants. Protests are raised that the leather guards are dangerous to base sliders, but the battered Bresnahan sticks by his armor.

1907 First batting cage is used by the Washington Senators.

The winningest family in baseball may have the 5 Delahanty brothers, who played in the early 1900s. Ed (the only Hall of Famer), Jim, Frank, Joe and Tom played a total of 41 years in the majors.

HISTORY OF PROFESSIONAL BASEBALL

Players

1903—NY's **Joe McGinnity** wins both ends of a
doubleheader 3 times in one month

1907—Philadelphia Phillies forfeit the opener after fans
throw snowballs at umpire **Bill Klem**

1908—**Fred Merkle,** Chicago Cubs, makes *Merkle's
Boner* in the race against the NY Giants by forgetting to
tag 2nd base and then heading for the clubhouse at
what seems to be the game's end

Records

1901—AL's **Irv Waldron** leads the year in at-bats, hitting
.311 and scoring 102 runs—and immediately disappears
from the baseball scene

1911—**Ty Cobb** leads the league in every offensive area
except home runs, and hits .420

1912—**Clyde Milan,** Washington Senators, steals 88
bases

NY Giant **Josh Devore** steals 4 bases in one inning

Business & Brass

1901—American League enters major league baseball

1902—*The National Commission,* a body of 3, is
established to govern baseball

1904—**Bill Yawkey** (future Red Sox owner **Tom
Yawkey's** foster father) buys the Detroit Tigers

1912—First team strike, in Detroit

Series, Pennants & All-Stars

1903—Pirate outfielder **Jimmy Sebring** hits the first
home run in the World Series

1905—**Christy Mathewson** of the NY Giants hurls 3
shutouts in 6 days against the Philadelphia A's

1911—First World Series game to be filmed for
commercial purposes

Rules & Equipment

1900—Width of home plate increases from 12" square to
a 17"-wide, 5-sided plate

1901—First 2 fouls become strikes in the National
League; AL follows in 1903

Baltimore Orioles dress in pink caps, black shirts, black
baggy pants, yellow belts and stockings and double
breasted jackets with yellow collars & cuffs

1903—The height of the pitcher's mound is limited to
15" above the level of home plate

1907—Giants catcher **Roger Bresnahan** invents
shinguards

1908—Pitchers are prohibited from scuffing or nicking
the ball

1909—Bunt foul on a 3rd strike becomes a strikeout

Firsts

1908—The Cleveland Naps lose a pennant by a half
game margin—the only team to do so

1915   **1920**   **1925**

1912—**Ty Cobb** is suspended from the AL indefinitely
after attacking a heckler in the NY stands

  1914—NY Giants outfielder **Red Murray** is knocked out
  by lightning while catching the game's last fly ball
  against Pittsburgh

    1918—Baseball stars **Ty Cobb**, **Herb Pennock** and
    Christy Mathewson enter the military

      1921—**Benny Kauff** of Brooklyn is banished for
      being of bad character

    1920—The Brooklyn Dodgers and Boston Braves battle
    for a record 26 innings

  1914—**Connie Mack** dismantles the champion A's
The Federal League enters major league baseball

    1916—Wrigley family enters baseball: **William Wrigley
Jr.** buys stock in the Cubs

      1919—Judge **Kenesaw Mountain Landis** becomes first
      Baseball Commissioner

      Giants **Hal Chase** and **Heinie Zimmerman** are thrown
      out for trying to fix games

      Chicago player **Chick Gandhil** and 7 others banned in
      the *Black Sox* scandal

        1920—Red Sox sell **Babe Ruth** to the Yankees
        for $125,000

          1922—The Supreme Court exempts baseball from
          anti-trust laws

          NY Giant *Shufflin Phil* **Douglas** is expelled from the
          leagues for writing a hate letter about **John McGraw**

            1924—Giants infielder **Jimmy O'Connell** and coach
            Cozy Dolan are ejected for arranging a $500 bribe for a
            Philadelphia player

1914—Boston's *Miracle Braves* sunk deep in the AL
basement on 18 July but zoom to the top in 10 weeks,
beating Philadelphia in the Series in 4 straight games

    1916—**Babe Ruth** pitches the longest winning Series
game: 14 innings

      1919—The Series increases to the best of 9 games (but
      not for long)

        1920—Cleveland Indian **Elmer Smith** socks the first
        Series grand-slam home run

          1922—Commissioner **K.M. Landis** is showered with ripe
          fruit after AL umpire **George Hildebrand** calls off a game
          due to darkness—with 30 minutes of daylight remaining

            1924—Washington wins its only World Series

              1925—**Roger Peckinpaugh** of the Washington Senators
              commits 8 errors—more than anyone in Series history

1911—Home teams begin wearing white uniforms to set
them off from visitors

    1918—**Bill Doak** of the St. Louis Cardinals invents a new
    cushioned glove with a built-up heel forming a V

      1920—Spitball is abolished

      New rabbit ball, made of strong Australian wool yarn,
      travels farther and bounces higher

          1926—Cork ball is introduced

1913—The NY Giants initiate public broadcasting by
attaching a microphone to home plate umpire **Charles
Rigler's** mask

    1920—Cleveland Indian **Ray Chapman** is killed by a
    pitch thrown by **Carl Mays** on 17 August

1925   1930   1935   1940

1936—In the first Hall of Fame vote, **Ty Cobb** is elected with 222 of 226 votes

1939—A pair of **Ty Cobb's** cleats becomes the first item in the Hall of Fame's collection of baseball paraphernalia

1942—In a letter to **Judge Landis**, President **Franklin Roosevelt** says that the country will benefit if baseball continues in spite of the war

1931—**Robert Moses** *Lefty* **Grove** of Philadelphia pitches a record 16 consecutive games

1938—**Johnny Vander Meer,** Reds, pitches 2 consecutive no-hitters

1926—**Ty Cobb** and **Tris Speaker,** player-managers of Detroit and Cleveland, are charged with fixing a game between their teams and are fired by team owners

1927—Trainer **Harrison J. *Doc* Weaver** joins the Cardinals and serves for 28 years. He invents a hand signal called the *inverted triple whammy*

1933—At age 30 **Tom Yawkey** becomes Red Sox owner

1937—Chicago Cubs give up $185,000 plus 2 pitchers and an outfielder for 27-year-old **Dizzy Dean** of the St. Louis Cardinals

1943—Night games banned due to wartime blackouts

St. Louis Cards advertise for players, after loaning many of their own to the war

1929—The Chicago Cubs lead 8-0 over Philadelphia in the 7th inning, so the crowd walks out...and misses the A's phenomenal 10-8 comeback

1931—At the Series, fans boo **President Herbert Hoover** and Prohibition, chanting *We Want Beer!*

1933—The first All-Star Game is held after Chicago Tribune sports editor **Arch Wald** suggests it should be a part of the city's Century of Progress exposition

1936—Braves Field in Boston draws the worst All-Star crowd ever—25,556—when fans mistakenly believe the game is sold out

1939—Yankee rookie **Charlie *King Kong* Keller** has a super Series: 3 homers, a triple, a double, 6 RBIs and a .438 average in the 4-game contest

1931—Sacrifice fly rule ends

Distance from plate to backstop shrinks from 90′ to 60′

1937—Umpires first use mud on baseballs to rough them up. One year later, the AL requires all umpires to prepare balls this way

1935—Baseball's first night game: Cincinnati Reds vs. Philadelphia Phillies at Crosley Field in Cincinnati. Reds win 2-1

1939—First televised game: Dodgers vs. Reds at Ebbets Field, on station W2XBS, New York

1945 **1950** **1955**

1946—AL teams try the *Williams Shift* to try to stop **Ted Williams'** hitting streak. They move the 3rd baseman near 2nd, the 2nd baseman near 1st, and 1st baseman to the foul line. It doesn't work.

1948—**Leo Durocher** coins the phrase *nice guys finish last* in reference to NY Giants manager **Mel Ott**

1949—Despite bone spurs on his heel, NY Yankee star **Joe DiMaggio** hits .346 to close out his career

1954—**Joe DiMaggio** marries actress **Marilyn Monroe**

1956—**Sal Maglie**, age 39, pitches a no-hitter for the Brooklyn Dodgers after being traded away by the Giants

1942—Cardinal **Mort Cooper** scores the first of 3 successive 20-win seasons

1947—The Giants finish only 4th but gather a record 221 homers

1944—Senator **A.B. *Happy* Chandler** of Kentucky becomes Commissioner

1946—**Bill Veeck** becomes president of the Cleveland Indians

1947—Brooklyn Dodgers manager **Leo Durocher** is suspended for an entire season for *conduct detrimental to the game* in connection with accusations that **Larry MacPhail**, NY Yankee co-owner, consorted with gamblers

1951—**Ford Frick** becomes Commissioner

1953—Boston Braves move to Milwaukee

Anheuser-Busch buys the St. Louis Cardinals

1954—**Walter Alston** becomes manager of the Brooklyn Dodgers

1944—St. Louis Browns win the pennant—their first in 5 decades

1945—The All-Star Game is abandoned: all the stars have gone to war

1947—Fans are given total control over All-Star selection until 1957, when Cincinnati fans stuff the ballot box

1947—**Jackie Robinson** becomes the first black in the World Series

1948—On a pick-off play at 2nd base, **Bob Feller** of Cleveland whirls around and throws to **Lou Boudreau**; ump **Bill Stewart** calls Boston's **Phil Masi** safe, and all hell breaks loose. The call is disputed to the present day

1950—Philadelphia's *Whiz Kids* wind down in the World Series, losing 4 in a row to the Yankees

1951—*Miracle of Coogan's Bluff* and the *Shot Heard 'Round the World*: **Bobby Thomson**, Giants, hits an unexpected home run into left field to win the NL Pennant

1950—Strike zone is lowered to between batters' armpits and top of knees; reversed in 1953; brought back in 1969

1954—Sacrifice fly rule is reinstated with a man scoring only after the catch

1947—**Jackie Robinson** becomes the first black to play for a major league team in the modern era

1955   1960   1965   1970

1962—Brothers **Hank** and **Tommie Aaron** each hit home runs in the same game 3 times in one year

1964—Baltimore's **Wally Bunker** wins 19 games as a 19-year-old

1967—Red Sox climb from last place to win the pennant

1961—Yankee **Roger Maris** hits his 61st homer, breaking Babe Ruth's 1927 record

1962—**Maury Wills** breaks **Ty Cobb's** base-stealing mark

1958—**Walter O'Malley** moves his Dodgers west to Los Angeles

1960—**Bill Veeck** installs the *exploding scoreboard* in Chicago

1961—**Charlie Finley** buys the Kansas City Athletics

1965—General **William D. Eckert** becomes Commissioner

1969—**Bowie Kuhn** becomes Commissioner

1970—Two-time Cy Young Award winner **Denny McLain** of the Detroit Tigers is suspended until mid-season, accused of involvement with bookie operations

1955—Dodgers grab their first Series title—over their arch rivals, the NY Yankees

1956—Yankee pitcher **Don Larsen** pitches a perfect Series no-hitter

1959—World Series record attendance reaches 420,784 as the LA Dodgers beat the Chicago White Sox

1960—Yankees set a number of Series team records— highest batting average (.338), most hits (91), most total bases (142), most runs (55), most runs batted in (54)— and then lose to the Pirates

1968—**Bob Gibson** of St. Louis strikes out 17 Detroit Tigers in the World Series

1971—Pittsburgh Pirate **Roberto Clemente** manages 2 homers, a triple, pair of doubles and 7 singles to help the underdogs triumph over Baltimore in the Series

1965—Houston Astrodome introduces artificial turf

1971—The major league requires protective at-bat helmets

Pittsburgh Pirates begin wearing double-knits with pullover tops

1973—AL introduces the designated hitter rule

First time that both league MVPs are 3rd basemen: **Ken Boyer** and **Brooks Robinson**

1975 **1980** **1985**

1972—Pittsburgh's **Roberto Clemente,** who holds the game's highest lifetime batting average at the time (.317) is killed in a plane crash while flying supplies to earthquake-stricken Nicaragua

1974—**Mike Schmidt** hits an apparent home run in the Astrodome—but the ball ricochets off a loudspeaker in center field

1979—Catcher **Thurman Munson,** an 11-year veteran with the NY Yankees, is killed while practicing takeoffs and landings in his private plane at the Canton OH airport

1973—**Nolan Ryan** beats **Sandy Koufax's** 382 season strikeout record. Number 383 was the last pitch of the season

1974—**Hank Aaron** breaks **Babe Ruth's** 714 lifetime home run record

1984—Expo **Pete Rose** makes his 4000th career hit. Only **Ty Cobb** ever exceeded that mark

1974—Yankee Stadium undergoes a $100 million facelift

1977—Texas Rangers' **Lenny Randle** is fined $10,000 during spring training for punching manager **Frank Lucchesi**

1981—Baseball strike forces a split season

1983—Scandal erupts as it is disclosed that numerous major league players have problems with drug addiction

1984—**Peter Ueberroth** takes over as commissioner

1976—Umpire **Bruce Froemming** ejects Yankee manager **Billy Martin** from a Series game for throwing a baseball and other things; fans go wild and police have to restrain them from taking the field

1978—**Reggie Jackson's** *hula act:* Trapped between 1st and 2nd base, Jackson appears to thrust out his hip; the ball hits him and bounces into left field, and the Yankees score a run

1980—The Philadelphia Phillies win their first Series in 97 years of NL play

1981—The LA Dodgers finally end their 4-Series losing streak, beating the rival Yankees

1974—Cowhide replaces horsehide as acceptable covering for baseballs

1974—Dodger relief pitcher **Mike Marshall** becomes the first relief man to win the Cy Young Award

1983—**Fred Lynn** of the Angels hits the first grand slam homer in All-Star history, leading to a 13-3 AL victory

PENNANT RACES

If only it wasn't for the damned Yankees!

Yankee lineups with nicknames like *Five O'Clock Lightening, Murderers' Row* and *Bronx Bombers* have dominated the AL pennant race for so long that other powerful teams find it hard to boast. Thirty-three American League championships have fallen to the club that began in 1903 as the New York *Highlanders* (that name came from the high ground they occupied at their 168th St. Hilltop Park; by 1905, *Yankees* had been coined and caught on as the new tag). Boston and the Philadelphia Athletics have won 9 pennants each; Detroit's Tigers have finished on top 8 times; and the Chicago White Sox and Baltimore Orioles have 5 crowns apiece. But the Yankees' consecutive pennant streaks are in a class by themselves: 3 straight flags (twice) in the 1920s; 4 straight in the 1930s; 5 straight (twice) in the late '40s; 4 straight in the '50s; 5 straight in the mid-'60s and 3 straight in the 1970s. In a 16-year period between 1949-64, they stepped to the front of the league 14 times.

The Yankees achieved this prominence with consistently stellar lineups, but students of Yankee history are inclined to pick the 1926-28 aggregation as the best baseball squad ever assembled—especially the 1927 lineup, which included **Earle Combs,** best lead-off man in the majors, who averaged .356 at bat; **Bob Meusel,**

.337 and 103 runs-batted-in; **Tony Lazzeri,** a .309, 102-RBI man; and **Waite Hoyt, Wilcy Moore, Herb Pennock** and **Urban Shocker,** a corps of pitchers that won a combined 78 games. To top it off, it had **Lou Gehrig,** driving in an immense 175 runs (he was to top this with a record 184 in 1931) off a .373 average and **Babe Ruth,** with 164 RBI and an unprecedented 60 home runs. These Yankees won 110 games for an AL record and swept the Pittsburgh Pirates 4 straight in the World Series.

What's left for the rest of the teams to claim? Well, in the National League, the Brooklyn/Los Angeles Dodgers have won 18 pennants, not bad at all. Back in 1906, the Chicago Cubs swamped the field with 116 season wins—still the big-league record. Cleveland's superb 1954 club, with **Bob Lemon, Early Wynn, Bob Feller** and **Mike Garcia** on the mound and with such swatters as **Larry Doby, Vic Wertz** and **Bobby Avila,** holds the AL record of 111 season victories—1 more than any Yankee team ever put together. In the past 14 years, the Oakland A's, victors in 3 straight pennant races, can claim almost as many championships as the Yankees. And Baltimore's Orioles actually have tied the vaunted Yanks for most flags over this period—4 for each.

WORLD SERIES

Can you imagine a World Series strung out over 15 games staged in barnstorming style in 10 cities over a month's time?

Modern club owners may be money-hungry, but they're perfectly reasonable compared to their forebears. In the late 1880s, the diamond tycoons spread post-season play over Michigan, Missouri, Illinois, New York, Pennsylvania, Massachusetts, Maryland *and* the District of Columbia. Baseball had the flavor of a vaudeville road race.

The real beginning of the Series is lost in the dimness of the past. Official records show the classic starting in 1903, but evidence of this widespread autumnal madness dates as far back as 1884.

Early Series
In 1882, a league called the **American Association** was formed. The established **National League** sneered at the AA upstart, calling it *bush* and *the beer and whisky league.* Millionaire brewer **Chris Von der Ahe,** owner of the St. Louis Browns of the new AA, declared the Nationals were cowardly in refusing to play his title-holding club. "Ve vill lick der stuffing out of dem if dey will face us!" boomed Von der Ahe. And so, in 1884, the rivals got together to kick off what became a wild, spike-tossing 7-year battle for the World Championship.

Althought the AA lost the first Series, Von der Ahe's Browns proceeded to beat the proud Nationals in at least one playoff and gained ties in 2 others. In '86, the upstarts downed the celebrated Chicago White Stockings, managed by **Cap Anson,** and won the crown. With a .442 batting average, the Browns' **Tip O'Neill** became the sport's newest luminary. The 1884-1890 Series,

which was an average of 8.1 games long, saved players who were paid $1500 to $2500 per season from starving. So happy was Von der Ahe at knocking off the arrogant Chicagoans that he donated his entire profit of about $15,000 to his athletes. That led to a division of the loot between other clubs and their players, often reaching $1000 per man. Results of the first 7 forgotten World Series:

1884 Providence Grays (NL) beat the New York Metropolitans (AA)
1885 St. Louis Browns (AA) played an undecided series with the Chicago White Stockings (who walked out in protest of an umpire's ruling)
1886 St. Louis Browns beat Chicago
1887 Detroit (NL) beat the Browns
1888 New York Giants (NL) beat the Browns
1889 Giants beat the Brooklyn Bridegrooms
1890 Louisville and Brooklyn played another undecided set of games

That merry era ended in 1890, when the American Association collapsed. (It was just as well that the AA failed, because by then so many crazies inhabited rosters that one player, after he was called out sliding, got a gun and shot the umpire. Irate Boston fans set fire to the bleachers in another year and the whole ballpark burned down. And this was only in league play!)

Replacing the AA in 1901 was the **American League.** Like the extinct AA, the AL was scorned by the elder National League. However, in 1903, owner **Barney Dreyfuss** of the NL champion Pittsburgh Pirates graciously agreed to an 8-game match with

Year	Season Games Won-Lost	American League	Series Games Won-Lost-Tied	National League	Season Games Won-Lost
1900				Brooklyn Dodgers	82-54
1901	83-53	Chicago White Sox		Pittsburgh Pirates	90-49
1902	83-53	Philadelphia A's		Pittsburgh Pirates	103-36
1903	91-47	**Boston Red Sox**	5-3	Pittsburgh Pirates	91-49
1904	95-59	Boston Red Sox		New York Giants	106-47
1905	92-56	Philadelphia A's	4-1	**New York Giants**	105-48
1906	93-58	**Chicago White Sox**	4-2	Chicago Cubs	116-36
1907	92-58	Detroit Tigers	4-0-1*	**Chicago Cubs**	107-45
1908	90-63	Detroit Tigers	4-1	**Chicago Cubs**	99-55
1909	98-54	Detroit Tigers	4-3	**Pittsburgh Pirates**	110-42
1910	102-48	**Philadelphia A's**	4-1	Chicago Cubs	104-50
1911	101-50	**Philadelphia A's**	4-2	New York Giants	99-54
1912	105-47	**Boston Red Sox**	4-3-1*	New York Giants	103-48
1913	96-57	**Philadelphia A's**	4-1	New York Giants	101-51
1914	99-53	Philadelphia A's	4-0	**Boston Braves**	94-59
1915	101-50	**Boston Red Sox**	4-1	Philadelphia Phillies	90-62
1916	91-63	**Boston Red Sox**	4-1	Brooklyn Dodgers	94-60
1917	100-54	**Chicago White Sox**	4-2	New York Giants	98-56
1918	75-51	**Boston Red Sox**	4-2	Chicago Cubs	84-45
1919	88-52	Chicago White Sox	5-3	**Cincinnati Reds**	96-44
1920	98-56	**Cleveland Indians**	5-2	Brooklyn Dodgers	93-61
1921	98-55	New York Yankees	5-3	**New York Giants**	94-59
1922	94-60	New York Yankees	4-0-1*	**New York Giants**	93-61
1923	98-54	**New York Yankees**	4-2	New York Giants	95-58
1924	92-62	**Washington Senators**	4-3	New York Giants	93-60
1925	96-55	Washington Senators	4-3	**Pittsburgh Pirates**	95-58
1926	91-63	New York Yankees	4-3	**St. Louis Cardinals**	89-65
1927	110-44	**New York Yankees**	4-0	Pittsburgh Pirates	94-60
1928	101-53	**New York Yankees**	4-0	St. Louis Cardinals	95-59
1929	104-46	**Philadelphia A's**	4-1	Chicago Cubs	98-54
1930	102-52	**Philadelphia A's**	4-2	St. Louis Cardinals	92-62
1931	107-45	Philadelphia A's	4-3	**St. Louis Cardinals**	101-53
1932	107-47	**New York Yankees**	4-0	Chicago Cubs	90-64
1933	99-53	Washington Senators	4-1	**New York Giants**	91-61
1934	101-53	Detroit Tigers	4-3	**St. Louis Cardinals**	95-58
1935	93-58	**Detroit Tigers**	4-2	Chicago Cubs	100-54
1936	102-51	**New York Yankees**	4-2	New York Giants	92-62
1937	102-52	**New York Yankees**	4-1	New York Giants	95-57
1938	99-53	**New York Yankees**	4-0	Chicago Cubs	89-63
1939	106-45	**New York Yankees**	4-0	Cincinnati Reds	97-57
1940	90-64	Detroit Tigers	4-3	**Cincinnati Reds**	100-53
1941	101-53	**New York Yankees**	4-1	Brooklyn Dodgers	100-54
1942	103-51	New York Yankees	4-1	**St. Louis Cardinals**	106-48
1943	98-56	**New York Yankees**	4-1	St. Louis Cardinals	105-49
1944	89-65	St. Louis Browns	4-2	**St. Louis Cardinals**	105-49
1945	88-65	**Detroit Tigers**	4-3	Chicago Cubs	98-56
1946	104-50	Boston Red Sox	4-3	**St. Louis Cardinals**	98-58
1947	97-57	**New York Yankees**	4-3	Brooklyn Dodgers	94-60
1948	97-58	**Cleveland Indians**	4-2	Boston Braves	91-62
1949	97-57	**New York Yankees**	4-1	Brooklyn Dodgers	97-57
1950	98-56	**New York Yankees**	4-0	Philadelphia Phillies	91-63
1951	98-56	**New York Yankees**	4-2	New York Giants	98-59
1952	95-59	**New York Yankees**	4-3	Brooklyn Dodgers	96-57
1953	99-52	**New York Yankees**	4-2	Brooklyn Dodgers	105-49
1954	111-43	Cleveland Indians	4-0	**New York Giants**	97-57
1955	96-58	New York Yankees	4-3	**Brooklyn Dodgers**	98-55
1956	97-57	**New York Yankees**	4-3	Brooklyn Dodgers	93-61
1957	98-56	New York Yankees	4-3	**Milwaukee Braves**	95-59
1958	92-62	**New York Yankees**	4-3	Milwaukee Braves	92-62
1959	94-60	Chicago White Sox	4-2	**Los Angeles Dodgers**	88-68
1960	97-57	New York Yankees	4-3	**Pittsburgh Pirates**	95-59
1961	109-53	**New York Yankees**	4-1	Cincinnati Reds	93-61
1962	96-66	**New York Yankees**	4-3	San Francisco Giants	103-62
1963	104-57	New York Yankees	4-0	**Los Angeles Dodgers**	99-63
1964	99-63	New York Yankees	4-3	**St. Louis Cardinals**	93-69
1965	102-60	Minnesota Twins	4-3	**Los Angeles Dodgers**	97-65
1966	97-63	**Baltimore Orioles**	4-0	Los Angeles Dodgers	95-67
1967	92-70	Boston Red Sox	4-3	**St. Louis Cardinals**	101-60
1968	103-59	**Detroit Tigers**	4-3	St. Louis Cardinals	97-65
1969	109-53	Baltimore Orioles	4-1	**New York Mets**	100-62
1970	108-54	**Baltimore Orioles**	4-1	Cincinnati Reds	102-60
1971	101-57	Baltimore Orioles	4-3	**Pittsburgh Pirates**	97-65
1972	93-62	**Oakland A's**	4-3	Cincinnati Reds	95-59
1973	94-68	**Oakland A's**	4-3	New York Mets	82-79
1974	90-72	**Oakland A's**	4-1	Los Angeles Dodgers	102-60
1975	95-65	Boston Red Sox	4-3	**Cincinnati Reds**	108-54
1976	97-62	New York Yankees	4-0	**Cincinnati Reds**	102-60
1977	100-62	**New York Yankees**	4-2	Los Angeles Dodgers	98-64
1978	100-63	**New York Yankees**	4-2	Los Angeles Dodgers	95-67
1979	102-57	Baltimore Orioles	4-3	**Pittsburgh Pirates**	98-64
1980	97-65	Kansas City Royals	4-2	**Philadelphia Phillies**	91-71
1981	59-48	New York Yankees	4-2	**Los Angeles Dodgers**	63-47
1982	95-67	Milwaukee Brewers	4-3	**St. Louis Cardinals**	92-70
1983	98-64	**Baltimore Orioles**	4-1	Philadelphia Phillies	90-72

Winners
Losers
*Game called on account of darkness

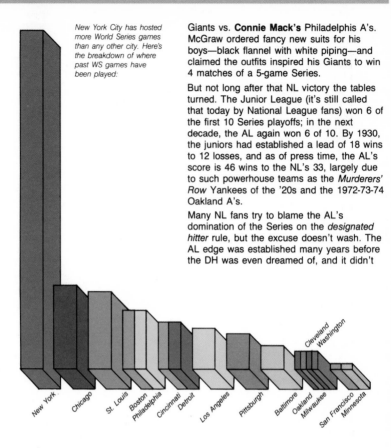

New York City has hosted more World Series games than any other city. Here's the breakdown of where past WS games have been played:

New York · Chicago · St. Louis · Boston · Philadelphia · Cincinnati · Detroit · Los Angeles · Pittsburgh · Baltimore · Cleveland · Washington · Oakland · Milwaukee · San Francisco · Minnesota

Giants vs. **Connie Mack's** Philadelphia A's. McGraw ordered fancy new suits for his boys—black flannel with white piping—and claimed the outfits inspired his Giants to win 4 matches of a 5-game Series.

But not long after that NL victory the tables turned. The Junior League (it's still called that today by National League fans) won 6 of the first 10 Series playoffs; in the next decade, the AL again won 6 of 10. By 1930, the juniors had established a lead of 18 wins to 12 losses, and as of press time, the AL's score is 46 wins to the NL's 33, largely due to such powerhouse teams as the *Murderers' Row* Yankees of the '20s and the 1972-73-74 Oakland A's.

Many NL fans try to blame the AL's domination of the Series on the *designated hitter* rule, but the excuse doesn't wash. The AL edge was established many years before the DH was even dreamed of, and it didn't

the AL champ Boston Pilgrims (who didn't become the Red Sox until 1907). A Beantown mob of 16,242 overfilled a park capable of holding only 10,000. In a mad scene, fans trampled outfield ropes and roamed the playing ground, chased by cops with billy clubs.

The incredible happened: Pittsburgh won 3 of the first 4 games! Featured was the first home run swatted in the World Series, by Pirates outfielder **Jimmy Sebring**. Then Boston roared back to take 4 straight games and the title. That 1903 clash, a huge upset, also introduced the first of many superstars who, mysteriously, played badly in the Series—the great **Honus Wagner** of Pittsburgh averaged only .222 with his mighty mace in this first modern World Series.

Growth
Between 1903 and today, baseball grew by leaps and bounds, becoming both popular and quite lucrative. Although attendance little more than tripled in 80 seasons (from 100,429 in 1903 to 338,981 in 1981), receipts went from $55,500 to nearly $6 million and the players' share increased from $32,612 to almost $2 million in the same time span. While a pioneer fan could buy a seat for 25 cents, millions now enjoy the games for free via TV and radio—which are the real sources of the modern game's wealth.

In 1904 the Series was washed out when **John T. *Tooth* Brush**, New York Giants president, and his manager, **John *Little Napoleon* McGraw**, snubbed the AL. "We wouldn't dirty our hands with that bunch," sneered Brush. Newspapers shouted protests, and so did the public. The next year, 1905, Series action resumed, with the strutting

appear in the Series at all until 1976. Even now, it's used only in alternating years, so it's certain that AL superiority hasn't depended on adding a 10th man to the lineup.

Records
When Yankee manager **Casey Stengel** first saw a rookie from Commerce OK lashing pitches over the fence, he knew immediately that the kid had it in his head and body to be one of the greatest. **Mickey Mantle's** record in World Series play may be his finest credential: the switch-hitting 200-lb blond slugged 18 home runs, drove in 40 runs and scored 42 runs—each an all-time WS record.

Mantle hit 3 homers in 3 Series (1956-60-64) and 2 round-trippers in 3 other post-season epics. It's true that he also struck out a WS record number of times—54—but that's the history of long-distance specialists. Despite a chronically bad leg, Mantle drove in 10 more WS runs than **Joe DiMaggio** and out-homered DiMag, 18 to 8, while appearing in just 2 more Series. And to think that the Yankees got Mickey Charles Mantle for a mere $1150 bonus!

Babe Ruth ranks second in WS homers, hitting 15 in 10 Series (2 fewer appearances than Mantle made). But they're about equal in HR production. Neither man averaged 2 homers per Classic; that honor is held by **Reggie Jackson** alone, who through 1981 had blasted 10 over the fence in just 5 Series. Some other Series records:

Most home runs in a single game:
3—Babe Ruth 1926, 1928
3—Reggie Jackson 1977

Most consecutive Series games with HRs:
4—Lou Gehrig 1928, 1932
4—Reggie Jackson 1977-78

Most games with more than 2 homers:
4—Babe Ruth, 1923-26-28-32

All-time batting average:
.418—Pepper Martin 1928-34
.391—Lou Brock 1964-68
.373—Thurman Munson 1976-78

Highest one-Series batting average:
In 1928, Babe Ruth ripped off 3 doubles, 3 home runs and numerous other hits for a fabulous mark of .625. No one has even come close to that in the past 55 years, though Hank Gowdy, Lou Gehrig, Johnny Bench and Thurman Munson have all passed the .500 mark (and Gehrig did it twice).

Most Series RBIs:
Yankees Mickey Mantle and Yogi Berra hold the records here. Mantle has 40 RBIs, with 41 runs scored; Berra is only one run and one RBI behind. But Berra is second to none in Series hits (71) and is tied for most doubles.

Pitching Wins:
10 wins in 11 Series games—Whitey Ford

Career Strikeouts:
94—Whitey Ford

Only No-Hit, No-Run Perfectly Pitched Game:
Don Larsen 1956

Pitcher With Highest Winning Percentage:
1.000 in 6 games—Lefty Gomez 1930s

Earned Run Average:
0.83—Harry Brecheen 1940s

Shutouts:
4—Christy Mathewson

Youngest Pitcher:
19 years—Ken Brett 1967

Youngest Pitcher to pitch a shutout:
20 years—Jim Palmer 1966

Oldest Pitcher:
46 years—John Quinn 1930

Youngest Non-Pitcher:
18 years—Freddie Lindstrom

Oldest Non-Pitcher:
42 years—Enos Slaughter 1958; Willie Mays 1973

Most Pitchers in 1 inning from 1 team:
5—Baltimore Orioles, in a futile attempt to stop the Pirates in the last inning of the 7th game 1979

Most Pitchers in 1 Game:
12—Cincinnati (against Boston) 1979

Dizzy Dean was among the first (and most notorious) of the many former pro players who took to announcing after retirement. He announced the Game of the Week on radio before going on to TV glory. With his fractured English, Dean was decried as "a horrible example to American schoolchildren" by teachers nationwide, and campaigns were launched to take him off the air because he mutilated the language so badly. A few sample Dizzyisms:

"He slud real good into second bag."
"This monkey thruns the balls so hard he might rupture hisself."
"Our engineer just got one atween the old eyeballs up here in the booth—a foul ball. He ain't ducked fast enough all season."
To his critics: "A lot of people who don't say ain't ain't eatin'."

Biggest WS flops by season's batting champs:
Ty Cobb, from .350 to .200, 1907
Chick Hafey, from .341 to .167, 1931
Bobby Avila, from .349 to .133, 1954

Steals:
14 in 3 Series—Lou Brock

Winningest Manager:
7 Series, 37 games—Casey Stengel, Yankees. But Joe McCarthy, an earlier Yankee boss, had a better percentage: 7 Series with only 2 defeats. Runners-up include Connie Mack (5 wins, 3 losses), Walter Alston (4-3), Miller Huggins (3-3) and John McGraw (4-6)

MVPs
When the Most Valuable Player of the World Series is selected, odds are that he'll be a dazzling infielder or hard-hitting outfielder, since the last 7 honorees have been from those categories. But it was just the opposite when the MVP award began in 1955: pitchers swept the voting for the first 5 years and then won 5 more awards between 1961-65. But things have changed: the last moundsman picked was **Rollie Fingers** of the 1974 Oakland A's. Here are all the MVPs:

Johnny Bench

Sandy Koufax

1955	**Johnny Podres**	Brooklyn Dodgers
1956	**Don Larsen**	New York Yankees
1957	**Lew Burdette**	Milwaukee Braves
1958	**Bob Turley**	New York Yankees
1959	**Larry Sherry**	Los Angeles Dodgers
1960	**Bobby Richardson**	New York Yankees
1961	**Whitey Ford**	New York Yankees
1962	**Ralph Terry**	New York Yankees
1963	**Sandy Koufax**	Los Angeles Dodgers
1964	**Bob Gibson**	St. Louis Cardinals
1965	**Sandy Koufax**	Los Angeles Dodgers
1966	**Frank Robinson**	Baltimore Orioles
1967	**Bob Gibson**	St. Louis Cardinals
1968	**Mickey Lolich**	Detroit Tigers
1969	**Donn Clendenon**	New York Mets
1970	**Brooks Robinson**	Baltimore Orioles
1971	**Roberto Clemente**	Pittsburgh Pirates
1972	**Gene Tenace**	Oakland A's
1973	**Reggie Jackson**	Oakland A's
1974	**Rollie Fingers**	Oakland A's
1975	**Pete Rose**	Cincinnati Reds
1976	**Johnny Bench**	Cincinnati Reds
1977	**Reggie Jackson**	New York Yankees
1978	**Bucky Dent**	New York Yankees
1979	**Willie Stargell**	Pittsburgh Pirates
1980	**Mike Schmidt**	Philadelphia Phillies
1981	**Ron Cey**	Los Angeles Dodgers
	Pedro Guerrero	Los Angeles Dodgers
	Steve Yeager	Los Angeles Dodgers
1982	**Darrell Porter**	St. Louis Cardinals
1983	**Rick Dempsey**	Baltimore Orioles

Although at times it seems that the American League owns the World Series, the National League often regains its honor at the All-Star Game in July.

Over the past 20 years, the NL has won 18 All-Star games; the AL took 2. Nothing else in the major leagues has ever been so lopsided. Between 1972-82, the NL won 11 consecutive meets; they win so consistently that one veteran American Leaguer, **Brooks Robinson,** said, "I played in 15 of the damned things for my league and 15 times we lost. What can I say? It's unbelievable."

Some insiders say that there may be too many *prima donnas* in the American loop who just don't care as much about the All-Star game as the other league's players do. Whatever the reason, it's still fun to watch the annual classic that was originated by **Arch Ward,** sports editor of the *Chicago Tribune,* back in 1933. Ward envisioned the first All-Star Game, a meeting of the best talent in each of the 2 leagues in a one-game duel, as a once-only affair held in conjunction with the Chicago Century of Progress Exposition of '33. But the game was so popular that it became a tradition. In 1959-62, baseball leaders experimented with 2 All-Star matches, but dropped the idea amid public disfavor.

With **Babe Ruth** hitting monster homers and playing stellar defense in right field, the AL took the 1933 inaugural game by 4-2. Since then, the game has generated some impressive records and high excitement:

Most games played—24 (Stan Musial, Hank Aaron, Willie Mays, all NL)
Highest batting average—.500 (Charlie Gehringer, AL)
Highest slugging percentage—.731 (Johnny Bench, NL)
Most extra-base hits—8 (Musial, Mays)
Most home runs—6 (Musial)
Most runs-batted-in—12 (Ted Williams, AL)
Most stolen bases—6 (Mays)
Most games pitched—8 (Jim Bunning, AL, Don Drysdale and Juan Marichal, both NL)
Most Strikeouts—19 (Drysdale)

MVPs

To be named **Most Valuable Player** in an All-Star extravaganza is enough to cap anyone's career. Since the first award was given in 1970, only one man—**Steve Garvey** of the NL—has been picked twice. **Gary Carter** of the NL is the only catcher ever to make it. The full roster of winners:

1970	**Carl Yastrzemski**	AL
1971	**Frank Robinson**	AL
1972	**Joe Morgan**	NL
1973	**Bobby Bonds**	NL
1974	**Steve Garvey**	NL
1975	**Bill Madlock**	NL
	Jon Matlack	NL
1976	**George Foster**	NL
1977	**Don Sutton**	NL
1978	**Steve Garvey**	NL
1979	**Dave Parker**	NL
1980	**Ken Griffey**	NL
1981	**Gary Carter**	NL
1982	**Dave Concepcion**	NL
1983	**Fred Lynn**	AL

NL	AL	All-Star Results		
		1933	AL 4	NL 2
		1934	AL 9	NL 7
		1935	AL 4	NL 1
		1936	NL 4	AL 3
		1937	AL 8	NL 3
		1938	NL 4	AL 1
		1939	AL 3	NL 1
		1940	NL 4	AL 0
		1941	AL 7	NL 5
		1942	AL 3	NL 1
		1943	AL 5	NL 3
		1944	NL 7	AL 1
		1945	no game	
		1946	AL 12	NL 0
		1947	AL 2	NL 1
		1948	AL 5	NL 2
		1949	AL 11	NL 7
		1950	NL 4	AL 3
		1951	NL 8	AL 3
		1952	NL 3	AL 2
		1953	NL 5	AL 1
		1954	AL 11	NL 9
		1955	NL 8	AL 5
		1956	NL 7	AL 3
		1957	AL 6	NL 5
		1958	AL 4	NL 3
		1959	NL 5	AL 4
			AL 5	NL 3
		1960	NL 5	AL 3
			NL 6	AL 0
		1961	NL 5	AL 4
			AL 1	NL 1
		1962	NL 3	AL 1
			AL 9	NL 4
		1963	NL 5	AL 3
		1964	NL 7	AL 4
		1965	NL 6	AL 5
		1966	NL 2	AL 1
		1967	NL 2	AL 1
		1968	NL 1	AL 0
		1969	NL 9	AL 3
		1970	NL 5	AL 4
		1971	AL 6	NL 4
		1972	NL 4	AL 3
		1973	NL 7	AL 1
		1974	NL 7	AL 2
		1975	NL 6	AL 3
		1976	NL 7	AL 1
		1977	NL 7	AL 5
		1978	NL 4	AL 3
		1979	NL 7	AL 6
		1980	NL 4	AL 2
		1981	NL 5	AL 4
		1982	NL 4	AL 1
		1983	AL 13	NL 3